MEMORY'S
ENCOURAGEMENT

MEMORY'S
ENCOURAGEMENT

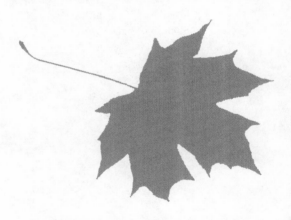

TONY GORRY

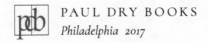

PAUL DRY BOOKS
Philadelphia 2017

First Paul Dry Books Edition, 2017

Paul Dry Books, Inc.
Philadelphia, Pennsylvania
www.pauldrybooks.com

ISBN 978-1-58988-121-1

For my wife, Anne,
and my daughters, April, Kate, and Meghan

I wish I could leave you certain of the images in my mind, because they are so beautiful that I hate to think they will be extinguished when I am. Well, but again, this life has its own mortal loveliness. And memory is not strictly mortal in its nature, either. It is a strange thing, after all, to be able to return to a moment, when it can hardly be said to have any reality at all, even in its passing. A moment is such a slight thing, I mean, that its abiding is a most gracious reprieve.

—*Gilead*, Marilynne Robinson

AMONG MY SOUVENIRS

I was running errands and, needing directions, I called up my car's navigator. "Turn left at the next intersection," she guided me; "proceed one-half mile." After shopping, I pressed the icon for my home. As my digital companion chimed in, I said, "Wait, I don't need your help to find my way back." Talking to a machine is something I do often these days. I closed the display. "Certainly I can remember where I've been." True in this case, but would I always find my way back home?

This talk with my machine made me think of another trip, one almost eight years ago: a return to my hometown to attend my fiftieth high-school reunion. My sixty-eighth birthday had been approaching, and the tug of nostalgia drew me back for the first time since that graduation. In anticipation, I rummaged through the contents of an old shoebox that had languished in the back of a closet for years. It held a motley collection of photographs, yellowed newspaper clippings, school programs, awards, and an old Bulova watch my father bought for me after he returned from the war.

The shoebox was a welcoming gateway to another country rich in presence. I felt immediately reconnected to places I'd lived and left long ago. My past emerged to prepare me for my homecoming.

I was struck by the way in which memory transformed time and space. I was there at my desk in 2008, but I was also in the world of my youth, many miles and decades away. I held a photograph taken at my grandmother's house, where I had lived while my father was fighting in Europe. It was probably 1944, and there I stood, almost four years old, with my wagon on the front porch. Though the picture was black and white, I knew that the wagon was red; my coat, blue; its six buttons, shiny brass. I could nearly smell the cool air of that spring day when sun-dappled snow still covered much of the ground.

In moments like this, I imagine myself a wanderer, one who has hurried along earlier pathways and now nears the end of his journey. I move more slowly, I take more breaks to ponder where I've been, to reflect on beautiful vistas of the past as well as rocky stretches, slippery crossings, and my wanderings off course—and the people I have met along the way. Remembrance pushes the present aside.

In a bookcase by my desk I have a copy of Homer's *Odyssey*, the story of another homecoming. With its nymphs, goddesses, and monsters, the epic is a catalog of delights and wonders. It is also an account of a harrowing voyage through danger, terror, and gloom. Odysseus has plundered the stronghold on the proud heights of Troy, and now Poseidon, enraged most recently by Odysseus blinding Polyphemus, the cyclops, resists the hero's return to Ithaca, where his wife and son have awaited his homecoming for twenty years.

Though my homecoming little resembled Odysseus's heroic journey, one of his encounters reminds me of our life in the digital age. During the penultimate leg of his journey, when Odysseus is adrift at sea, Poseidon blasts his raft. Clinging to wood from the wreckage and barely escaping drowning, Odysseus washes up on shore, naked and exhausted. After a night's sleep, he awakes in confusion. What place is this? Who lives here? How will they receive him?

His questions are answered when he meets Nausicaa, the daughter of the king in this land of Scheria. It is, she says, a place distant from other lands. Its inhabitants, the Phaeacians, are dear to the immortal gods. Indeed, the Phaeacians often encounter Olympians strolling in their midst.

Concerned that she might be seen unchaperoned with a naked stranger, Nausicaa sends Odysseus on alone to her father's palace. There Homer reveals an otherworldly stamp on Phaeacian buildings and crafts. The palace is a marvel, airy and luminous, with the luster of the sun and moon. Bronze-paneled walls with azure moldings of lapis lazuli lead to the reception hall where the post and lintel are silver on silver and where gold handles curve on the doors. The entrance is flanked by hounds sculpted from silver and gold. Odysseus learns that Poseidon has made the Phaeacian ships as "swift as a wing or a thought." They need neither pilot nor rudder to travel miraculous distances and still return in a single day.

A large garden fronts the Phaeacian palace. There the interpenetration of the heavenly and the mundane is striking. Apples, pears, figs, olives, and grapes grow profusely, giving their bounty regardless of season. As he scans this wondrous garden, Odysseus sees clusters of green grapes, others still ripening on the vine, some drying in the sun, and still others being crushed for wine. While currants dry in one part of the garden, vintners tromp purple grapes in another, and in yet another the new grapes are just losing their blossoms. It is not only the materiality of Scheria that has been touched by the gods. Time, too, has been transformed. In this garden the past, present, and future commingle. Yet despite these marvels, nostalgia retains its grip on Odysseus. He yearns for Ithaca, his wife and son.

The Scherian garden may be just poetic fancy, but my garden of the past is unworldly in its own way. There I cultivate remembrances and shape what I know about the past. In reverie I construct personal edifices, some gleaming, others shadowed. In memory, what was long ago can suddenly be close at hand; what was far, now near. A strange garden, with its own strange physics, but one I lately tend with care, for its produce enriches and encourages me.

Odysseus had been away for twenty years when a god-powered ship whisked him to Ithaca to complete his homecoming. What would he find changed on his return? How would the world for which he yearned greet him?

Digital technology has ushered many of us into its own otherworldly place. Kevin Kelly calls it the "Eden of everything." At the speed of thought we traverse electronic byways. All places and all knowledge are a click away. Flitting from one encounter to another, we revel in our ability to juggle several tasks and encounters, gaining from each just enough, just in time. Engaging constructions draw our attention. They call us to stay, to explore, to wonder at their ever increasing magnificence. For many, the call of home is weakening.

I find myself immersed in this digital world, living more on the screen than I would have thought possible when I began my professional career in computer science nearly five decades ago. Digital technology has thrust us into the fast lane. While I have been excited to be a guest in what David Brooks calls "the greatest cocktail party ever," lately I've been nostalgic for times and places past.

The word "nostalgia" suggests a Greek ancestry, but it is a portmanteau forged in the seventeenth century by a Swiss doctor, combining the Greek words *nostos*, for "returning," and *algos*, for "pain." It described the condition afflicting soldiers as they left their homes and entered foreign lands. Reminders of home, such as smells or sounds, were enough to turn fighting men haggard and ineffectual.

Assuming the problem was physiological, physicians of the time used leeches, opium, and visits to Alpine retreats to rid sufferers of their affliction. In modern times, nostalgia has been recognized as an ailment not of the body, but of the mind. At my desk, faced with a glowing screen, at times I feel like an immigrant to a new country, still yearning for my homeland. In the midst of the electronic wonders, an artifact, a book, or even a conversation may suddenly call me to cross the border into my native land.

The route from the airport to my hometown is well marked, one I could easily follow with or without a digital assistant. But what guide did I have through the decades that had passed? Could I trust my recollections? Jane Austen's Fanny said memory is "sometimes so retentive, so serviceable, so obedient; at others, so bewildered and so weak; and at others again, so tyrannic, so beyond control." As I sifted through the contents of my shoebox, I wondered about the family lore handed down over the years. How much was recollection and how much was invention? We form memories in haste, encoding experiences as sparse constellations of authentic details, and a variety of psychological factors may later combine to alter what we remember. Careful testing of people with so-called autobiographical memories, those who can seemingly remember every day of their lives, reveals that even they mix facts with conjecture in what they recall. Surely I have invented some of what I remember.

Walter Benjamin said we should approach our buried past like archaeologists, returning again and again to the same matter; to scatter it as one scatters earth, to uncover long-sought secrets that yield only to the most meticulous investigation. But more than excavation is needed. What are we to make of the objects we uncover? By themselves, they tell us nothing, as would be the case in a gallery that displayed them with no dating, commentary, or context. It is only when we embed them in narrative that they acquire voice.

Humans are born with an avidity for stories; I live in them and for them. Through storytelling I empathize with my family and neighbors, even with people I've never met. Gossip, for example, serves practical needs such as monitoring group activity, maintaining hierarchy, and promoting bonding, but many of us so enjoy talking about others, we even gossip about people we do not know, imagining their lives for our own pleasure.

We tell ourselves stories to make sense of our past and current place in the world. Recalled stories commingle imagination and emotion. Some may seem immutable, as though set in a psychological stone to which Benjamin might have us take a pickaxe. Others, as I have learned, are working drafts, amenable to editing and reformulation. With these, like the novelist, we may involve an artistic license to alter duration, order, and even causality. We may also encounter stubborn facts and circumstances, which in dreams we evade, but not in recall.

In this memoir I've included stories of my childhood, even as today I live in the Eden of everything where machines are altering my relation to what has gone before. Among these memories I have added reflections on the ways in which seeing through the surface of the present to the depths of the past has enriched my life and sustained me in some difficult times.

As I settled to my writing, I noticed some loose change lying on my desk. Other coins are likely in my briefcase or in cupholders, ignored or forgotten. While a few lost cents may be of little consequence, nickels, dimes, quarters, and bills can be caught up for later use. It would be a shame to waste that money.

But time is the true currency of my life. Without it, money would be worthless. And time can't be saved for later. My life produces no loose change. Moments of absorption, joy, or sorrow are spent in their entirety. In the few minutes between meetings, a wait for an elevator, a stop at a traffic light, or a lull in a conversation— time slips away. Tennessee Williams claimed "that life is all memory, except for the one present moment that goes by you so quick you hardly catch it going," to which we return again and again.

So it's not time I hoard, but memories, to which, like a miser, I return to inspect and embellish. I may stumble upon some that, like rediscovered coins, have lain hidden for years. Then I've found that, while the value of a found nickel is still five cents, the worth of a recollection may increase greatly in the mysterious economy of my memory.

HOMECOMING

I drove away from the Albany airport, heading north to my hometown, Glens Falls, and the lake, places of my childhood. I cruised along the Northway, then exited on a narrow road that curled around the southern end of the lake. I pulled over to take in the view. More houses, more boats on the lake, and the blue expanse was even grander than I remembered. Ripples and small waves ruffled the water. After a minute, I took a deep breath and continued driving, the road no longer dirt as I remembered, but paved, probably for years. Soon I was in the Knob. At least, I was where the Knob had been years ago. The abutment into the water, where the Ice House had stood, was covered by a restaurant and marina. Behind me, on the side of the road away from the lake, an array of houses dotted what had been the fields that lay at the foot of Buck Mountain.

I parked alongside a knoll and noticed a low bench with a dedication carved into its back. I recognized a family name long associated with the Knob, but the given names meant nothing to me. Sitting on the bench, I saw the lake spreading out behind the marina. Boats threw up wakes as they swooped in to drop water skiers in the shallow water. Farther out, a catamaran crossed the bay. When I was a child, the residents drank water straight from the lake. I never again tasted water so pure.

The lake glittered under the rays of the setting sun, the undersides of leaves turned translucent reds and oranges. A short distance down the other side of the road, a man standing by a smoldering pile of leaves stirred them occasionally with a rake. His prodding caused brief flare-ups, which after a few seconds scented the air around my bench.

THE ICE HOUSE

It's a late summer afternoon in 1945. A male deer is leading two females along a switchback on the side of Buck Mountain in the Adirondacks in upstate New York. They're halfway across the last turn when the sharp crack of a rifle splits the air. The buck stops abruptly, standing rigidly in the soft light. The does freeze as well. For some moments, only his ears and nostrils move. Then he shakes himself, sending a ripple under his coat from his neck to his haunches. He snorts, and turns from the trail onto a narrow rocky track hidden by bushes. The inner side of the path clings to the mountain, but the outer edge drops off sharply to the valley below. The buck and his companions clatter out along the ridge. As they round a bend, the buck again stops. Standing still, he surveys the vista of the lake laid out below. The females fidget, awaiting his direction. Twenty seconds later, he snorts once more and starts up again. The three deer round the bend and are soon gone.

As the second doe makes the final turn, one of her back hooves dislodges a small rock, sending it spinning over the edge of the trail to carom down the hill. It flickers as the fading light catches a polished side. The rock glances off a large boulder and spins sharply off course. It bounces twice, once left, once right, into a patch of moss-covered stones. It strikes the edge of a large tree root, seems to poise for a moment, and finally nestles into a depression among mottled leaves.

Below the deer, between the mountain and the lake, lies the Knob, a loose cluster of summer cottages and permanent homes, sited on an abutment into Lake George. Only a few hardy souls live in the Knob during the region's harsh winters, but in summer, the cottages are filled with families drawn by the swimming, boating, hiking, and sheer beauty of the lake. During the war years it is mostly mothers who bring their children, seeking a few days break from work and from loneliness and fear for their husbands overseas.

The Ice House is the gravitational center of the Knob. Flanked by boat slips and a gas station, it stands by the packed dirt road that edges the lake. It's festooned with hand-painted signs, proclaiming "Beer, Pop, and Pinball" and "Honest Weights and Square Trade." During winter, workers with pick axes and ripsaws cut out blocks of snowy ice from the lake and pack them in a windowless cellar in back. Covered with burlap and sawdust, the ice lies for months in the dark room, waiting for delivery to neighboring houses and cottages when summer arrives.

In summer, visitors and residents find their way to the Ice House daily. Some come for ice, but they also come seeking bait, ammunition, beer, cigarettes, and newspapers. One chalkboard lists prices for fresh caught fish; another, the prices for vegetables. At dawn, deer can be seen drinking from the lake behind the Ice House before they retreat to refuge on the eponymous mountain. These days, there is almost continuous conversation about the war. Exchanges that in the previous years had been laden with gloom are now lightened by news of allied advances in Europe and the Pacific. Still, some whose husbands or sons have not yet returned avoid any talk of the conflict.

With so many fathers at war, stays in the cottages are short; many of the women work, but because the Knob is less than ten miles from town, a mother might bring her children several times over the course of the summer. A group of women would shepherd a gaggle of energetic kids for a visit. Here they relax, and their children rejoice in exploration and modest adventure.

Older residents of the Knob can usually be found seated along the counter that serves as an informal bar inside of the Ice House. Through the long summer days, the owner sells six-ounce bottles of cream soda, Lithiated Lemon, and Coke, chilled in a tub of icy water. Late in the afternoon, he adds bottles of Dobler beer.

For the kids the Ice House is a great lure, even though the sawdust on the walks and floor grinds into their bare feet. Outside they can cool off on a burlap-covered block of ice, set for delivery. Inside they get to "Shoot the Jap!" at the pinball machine which sits against a back wall.

At the end of the machine, a glass-fronted box encases a painted jungle scene, perhaps copied from a Rousseau painting. Instead of a tiger in the grass, however, this painting shows a man with a machine gun crouching in the grass. In front of this picture, back and forth, a Japanese soldier struts from one side of the box to the other. He jerks his arm spasmodically, as though he'd been trained by Nazis. Under a black mustache, his teeth protrude, making him look like a Nazi gerbil. To resolve any questions regarding his true nature, he carries a sword in one hand and a Japanese flag in the other. The object of the game is to kill him.

His chances of escape are slim indeed. He's been killed many times before. It's not the gun mounted on far end of the box that does him in. That's solely decorative. Rather, it's a shiny ball rolling down a slope through a maze of holes and bumpers that determines his fate. Thumps on the sides of the box urge the ball toward a special hole—the Hole to Hell. But the soldier doesn't die easily. Sometimes the ball seems to have a mind of its own. It bounces erratically from side to side, from bumper to bumper, as it rolls down the slope. It may pass by that dark hole. Then he will escape death. More often, though, the ball falls in. Then a bell clangs, and he dies once more, slumped midway along his run. Those who have killed him cheer.

Adults often try their hand, some several times a day. Occasionally one who successfully shoots him mutters, "Gotcha, you yellow bastard!" or "Take that, asshole!"

During the bitterly cold days of February, 1945, only regulars can be found at the Ice House. Some buy bait for ice fishing. Others are gathered for coffee and gossip and to once again kill that lone enemy soldier. With no children around, they can give full voice to their contempt for the pinball machine's buck-toothed figure. Curses unsuitable for the ears of kids often fill the air.

While the war in Europe seems resolved, the push across the Pacific continues. So an undercurrent of worry persists. A number of local boys have returned; some have been wounded, some have passed through the hell of battle unscathed. Throughout February and into March, attention focuses on Iwo Jima, where the Allies confront bitter resistance from the entrenched enemy. Newspapers recount the assault as the two forces contest the mountainous terrain, seemingly foot by foot. The photograph of the flag raising on Suribachi at the end of the month bolsters spirits.

In the Knob, however, joy is tempered by the knowledge that one of their own is fighting with the Marines on Iwo Jima, where casualties are reported to be frightfully heavy. That joy is extinguished altogether two weeks later when a dreaded telegram arrives. Rob Wilson has been killed in action.

Rob's parents, Marge and Tom, have run the gas station next to the Ice House for many years. Until he was called to war, Rob worked at both places whenever he had time off from school. In winter he cut blocks of ice, in summer he delivered them to houses and cottages around the Knob. Everyone knew him. Everyone cared for him. Now everyone mourns him.

In late June, women and children begin to return to the cottages at the Knob. Some of their husbands have returned to join them, eager to put behind the horrors and loneliness of recent years. The Ice House becomes a stage on which the wonderful return to the ordinary plays out.

But there are no parts in this play for Marge and Tom Wilson. They busy themselves with the gas station, and they often drop in for coffee or beer at the Ice House, but they are like actors reading for parts they know they will never win. Those who have known them for years attend carefully to their own performances, hoping in time that grief will loosen its hold on Tom and Marge.

Yet the kids are immersed in the freedom and adventure of summer. Subtle aspects of adult behavior pass over them like a light breeze, only occasionally diverting them from their activities. "Shoot the Jap!" still appeals to them, particularly to those kids visiting the Knob for the first time. Even after the climactic bombs end the Japanese threat, the pinball machine attracts many. By implicit agreement, it is not put in play when Tom and Marge are around.

One day in August, Rob's parents are drinking coffee with friends at the counter in the Ice House when some kids burst in to announce that a visitor is looking for them. The swinging doors open to reveal a young, uniformed Marine. Stepping inside, he immediately sees the pinball machine. He stands still, staring at the Japanese soldier, who is slumped unmoving at the midpoint of his track.

A tug at his sleeve startles him, and one of the kids directs the Marine to Tom and Marge. He removes his hat and crosses the sawdust-covered floor with a noticeable limp. Standing stiffly before the couple, he introduces himself as one of Rob's buddies. He tells them that he'd had been through a lot with Rob, including the long struggle on Iwo Jima. Patting his leg, he recounts how he'd been wounded on what proved to be the final day of the battle. Rob had gotten through it all with only scrapes and bruises. The day after Suribachi had been taken, the men had been lying around on the slope, exhausted by their efforts of the previous days. Rob announced he had to clean up. He'd poured some water from his canteen into his helmet and was fumbling in his pack for an old razor when an enemy soldier burst out of a brush-covered hole on the hillside, screaming and firing his rifle. "Our guys shot him," the Marine says softly, "but not before that bastard killed Rob. Shot him in the head."

Their visitor chokes. He can't say more. Marge and Tom sit in stunned silence. It is as if their son has just died a second time.

One afternoon, near the end of the summer, the kids are leaving the Ice House after a day of swimming, tag, sodas, and shooting the Jap. One spots something glinting in the grass by the edge of the walk: a rifle shell. The kids have often seen spent rifle shells, which are relics of deer hunting. They collect the empty casings to use as money in their card games. But this shell is different; it hasn't been fired. Its head still protrudes from the case. It's no artifact, they realize, but a real bullet. Having shown it quickly around, the boy puts it in his pocket, out of grown-up sight.

After supper, the kids gather to ponder the fate of the bullet. Early opinions incline toward giving the bullet to an adult. They know it is a dangerous thing. But when one of the girls suggests "launching it like a rocket," new prospects open. But how to launch it without a gun? After inventing and discarding several complex methods, they decide they could throw it hard, butt-first, onto cement. That might work. That becomes the plan.

With school in the offing, tomorrow is the last day at the Knob for many of them. While their parents are packing, the kids assemble at the Ice House just before dusk. They bring the bullet. The concrete path that runs between the Ice House and the gas station extends into small parking lot at the back of the two buildings. There, with an old broom, they sweep sawdust away to clear a small circle on the cement. Spacing themselves on its circumference, they wait. When he is sure no adults are in sight, the caretaker produces the bullet. Holding it aloft, he steps into the circle, chants what he takes to be a magic charm, and hurls the bullet straight down. The other kids wince and turn away. But the bullet just bounces several times and rolls toward one of them who in turn, throws it onto the cement with the same result. Laughter and excitement rise. New magic charms are proposed. Others want to try their hands.

Tom Wilson is straightening up in the back of the gas station, a job Marge would ordinarily handle. But she isn't up to much these days. Neither is he, but at least he can shuffle along with the routine. Tom hears the noises of the kids and, through the curtains on the back door, sees the quick rising and falling of their hands. Curious, he opens the door and steps out.

The unmistakable crack of a rifle shot rips the late afternoon stillness. It must be close by, Tom thinks, searching around frantically. But he sees no gun. The pitch of the children's screaming rises sharply. They twist about in agitation—or in agony? Seeing nobody but the kids in their writhing circle, Tom stumbles forward and clutches the closest, who tries to squirm away. Tom finds no blood. He lets the boy go and grabs a girl who is jumping around near by. Again, no apparent harm. And the others are too active to have been shot. As Tom lunges about among the kids, he pieces together the story of the bullet launch. He begins to moan, first softly, then more loudly. His harsh, raspy gasping brings the kids to a halt in a ragged circle around him. He tries to speak, but is unable to still his sobbing. He falls to his knees. Finally, he is able to croak "crazy kids" and "stupid," but sobs again overcome him.

The kids stare at him, transfixed by such strange adult behavior. Finally, one of the kids breaks the spell and retreats furtively over the sawdust and down the walk. The others join an accelerating flight. But before they round the corner of the Ice House, many turn to look back once more. For a long time after their nervous laughter and the slapping of their bare feet have faded, Tom sits shuddering in the circle of sawdust.

The deer have settled in their meadow high up on the mountain. From there, the view affirms the locals' claim that theirs is one of the world's most beautiful lakes. Certainly a match for Lake Geneva, although they know that lake only from some old picture postcards. Indifferent to the panorama, the deer browse contentedly as the sun begins to set.

THE COOKIE JAR

When I arrived for the reunion, the center of town sported a new traffic circle and some refurbished older buildings, but I was staying on a street with the pleasant, slightly scruffy houses of my childhood. During the next few days, I took breaks from the reunion to wander the parts of town I had once known so well. My grandmother's clapboard house, once gray, was now dusky blue. It had seemed grand, now it was modest, but its prominent porch, sprawling lawn, and irregular garden fronted by an iron gate were little changed. I could see what might still be a window to the kitchen. There would have been the jar that my aunt sometimes filled with her chocolate cookies. The smell pervading the house always alerted me. When Aunt Barbara intended the cookies for neighbors, she put a "Do Not

Touch" sign next to the jar. Ah, surely she won't miss one, I thought one summer day when the aroma called. That cookie was so good. But heading for the back door, I ran into my aunt.

"Hey! Have you been into my cookies?"

"Oh, no. I saw the note," I declared, head down, studying something on my shoe.

"Well, seeing is believing," she rebuked me. "Go play outside—and leave my cookies alone."

As I passed the mirror in the back hall, I caught a glimpse of a boy whose mouth was smeared with chocolate.

Indeed, seeing is believing. But standing before the old gate, so many years later, I decided it goes the other way, too. Believing is seeing. In the present, and in the past, as well.

FALLING LEAVES

It's a Saturday afternoon in October 1935. Two men walk along Sherman Avenue, a quiet elm-lined street. Above them, the trees' long branches frame a roof of leaves which is an almost impenetrable green in summer, but now, skeleton-like, shows a fading sky. I follow the two in memory, passing silently and effortlessly through the trees.

Leaves mottle the street, the sidewalk, and the adjoining yards. Someone has raked heaps of them up near the curb. As the two men walk, one man puffs a pipe, and the other takes intermittent drags on a cigarette. Their smoke drifts up into air scented by the earlier burning of piles of leaves. Decades later, I can almost smell it.

George, the pipe smoker, has walked this street many times. Three blocks ahead is the house where he was born and, except for his time in college, has always lived. As a child he jumped into leaf piles along this way, rolling around to emerge with his hair a tangle of leaves and twigs. At home, his mother laughed at the sight of him, although later she grumbled a bit as she worked to clean his curly hair. On this day, most of the hair is gone. A porkpie hat hides what little remains. The spring that had propelled him joyously into leaf piles has deserted him. I see him walking heavily, old beyond his years, as he shuffles toward his home.

Cigarette-smoking Flash is a head taller. And younger, but not as much as their appearances suggest. Slim, jacketed in leather, he occasionally stirs the leaves or kicks a stone he uncovers. When his natural, more vigorous pace moves him a few yards ahead, he pauses to look around. This is new territory for him. Until a week ago, he lived in Ohio. Here the houses are old Victorians, larger than those back home. Some have expansive front porches. But they are generally worn and occasionally shabby. As in Ohio, upkeep has been undermined by dreary economics. At one house, a concrete statue of an angel seems to draw itself back into the bushes. At another, leaves float in an abandoned rubber wading pool near the sidewalk. But at every third or fourth house, people come and go in activities of a late autumn afternoon. Not so different from Ohio after all.

Laughing and gesturing as they amble along, the two walkers might be old friends. Yet they met less than two hours ago, brought together by beer and peanuts at the Commodore Club. A popular gathering place for a decade, the club had a front door, but few patrons entered that way. Most came through a small parking lot behind the club that served a hardware store and a bakery as well. A small neon sign promised a bar at the Commodore. Long-standing habit brought George to the club on his walk home from work at the insurance company, and Flash was wandering about the neighborhood of his hotel when he saw the neon invitation. Like George, he could use a beer.

The two now sit at the bar, separated by an empty stool and a dish of peanuts. They absently reach for a few nuts. A slight collision, quickly followed by a duet of "No, go ahead," sets them to talking.

"You must be new in town," grunts George.

"Right," says Flash, studying his beer. Then, as though having made a decision, he continues, "Just in yesterday from Ohio. Looking at a new job here. For a meat-packing company. I'm George, but my friends call me Flash. What's your name?"

"Why, it's George, too. I'm an actuary at the insurance company down by the river." He pauses, then pushes on, "Seems like I've worked there forever, but these days, I'm glad to have a job. I don't know about Ohio, but there's not much doing here. My sisters had their hours cut back, and my brother had to go to Utica to get work. I'm surprised you've got something new in town."

"Actuary, huh? You must have a big brain," laughs Flash shaking his head. "Well, I hope my deal works out."

He drags the intervening stool aside, angling himself more directly to George. His companion is red-faced with a ragged mustache.

"So what's it like to live here?" Flash asks. "Pretty

cold in the winter, I've heard. We get some hard winters back home, but not like here."

"Well, I've lived here all my life—except for college. So, I'm used to the seasons. In fact, I've lived all my life in the same house. College hardly counts as time away. My brother Frank was a year ahead of me there and two of my sisters were at a women's college nearby. It was like I took my family with me. I guess you could say I never left home."

Over second beers and shared peanuts, the local and newcomer continued a congenial back and forth about themselves, and life here and back in Ohio.

"London's my hometown, outside Columbus," contributes Flash, "much smaller than this place. When the time came, I was really ready to go to college. Had a great time. Made lots of friends. Played football, pretty well as a matter of fact. Got to see my name in the news-papers—George the Flash, that was me."

He scoops up some more peanuts and counts them out on the bar as he continues. "But then hell broke loose with the stock market and all. My father lost his business and most of his money. No medical school for me. Off to the meat-packing plant—hog disassembly we called it."

"Shame," mumbles George.

"Oh, lots of people had it worse, I know. My dad for one, poor old guy," says Flash. "But I turned out to be a good salesman. That's how I escaped the plant. I've been a traveling salesman for them the past few years. Now they want me to open new territory here in the northeast."

"Are you married? Kids?" George inquires.

"No, no," Flash responds. "No luck so far. How about you?"

"I've got a dog. That's about it." Both Georges laugh.

"I think you'll like it here," George goes on. "Do you like fishing, hunting, outdoor stuff?"

"Fishing, for sure," says Flash. "I don't know about hunting. I don't think I'm much with guns. But I suppose I can give it a try."

"I'm like you," George nods. "I've got fly-fishing gear, which I use a lot. But I never use the shotgun my father left to me."

Suddenly, George looks at his watch. Dinnertime is fast approaching.

"Say, Flash—I can call you that, right? Why don't you come to my house for dinner? My two sisters—both single," he says with a smile, "and my mother will be there. I'm sure they'd be glad for you to join us."

"Sure, call me Flash. By God, that's great, George. Thanks. I'll take your word that I won't be a nuisance."

George smiles, and the two of them set off on their walk along Sherman Avenue to the gray clapboard house. As I have many times before, I follow and know what is in the offing.

At the sound of the door, George's mother greets them. "Why, George, who's this you've got with you?"

I feel I have slipped past them into the house and am now hidden in the shadows.

George briefly recounts the meeting at the Commodore, while Ma takes Flash's arm, welcoming him more as a regular than a stranger unexpectedly arrived for dinner. Patting his hand, she retreats to the kitchen from which wafts the aroma of roasting pork.

George leads Flash to the living room where two women sit on a sofa talking. After his quick introduction of Flash, they're as welcoming as Ma.

"From Ohio?" laughs Barbara, with a nice smile and perhaps a few years younger than Flash. "You're a long way from home. What brings you here?"

He briefly tells of the assignment that brought him to town.

"So here you're all alone," notes Helen. "If our other brother and our other two sisters were here, you'd really be outnumbered. As it is, you'll have to contend with just the three of us—and, of course, Ma." She is taller than Barbara, and Flash judges her probably a year or two older. He'd never been much good at guessing women's ages. He is, however, good at judging what he thinks of as quality: some ineffable amalgam of beauty, intelligence, humor, and vitality. I know that Helen will rise rapidly in his esteem as the evening progresses.

While George gets drinks and snacks for Flash and himself, Jake, his brown and white cocker spaniel, roused from his sleep, patrols for pieces of cracker.

The sisters attend to Flash's story as though it were a report from another planet. Barbara shudders as he leads them through the process of hog disassembly that put pork in their oven. Helen surprises and pleases him with a few questions about plant operations. Later, at the table, he chides Barbara gently for eating the poor porker. Then, no more references to hogs.

For a short time, Ma holds court. Until his death some six years earlier, her husband had been a prominent businessman, who was interested in new things. The house, she notes with obvious pride, was the first in town wired for electricity. Glancing about, Flash detects signs of disrepair. He tells of his own father, who died four years before. He'd owned a candy store, and Flash proceeds with considerable success to guess the favorite candy of each of his dinner companions. Chocolate covered almonds for Helen. Right, she exclaims. Barbara smiles. She's never seen her sister eat one.

Was it love at first sight? Or that last beer? Whatever it was, as he is leaving, Flash abruptly draws Helen aside.

"Helen, I'm going to marry you," he blurts out, loud enough for all to hear.

They laugh at what they take to be another of Flash's jokes. Helen blushes. She holds his arm for a long moment. She looks steadily into his eyes. She says nothing.

Flash is serious, despite having met her only a few hours before. And persuasive, too. In three months, he and Helen, my parents, will marry. The audacious pronouncement, the proposal the next week, and the marriage quickly following make a story that for more than fifty years casts a romantic light on their union. Uncle George often tells the tale, emphasizing his role as matchmaker. A couple of hours at the bar, a couple more at dinner, and then a wedding. All because of him!

For several months after their marriage, Helen and Flash live in the house on Sherman Avenue, while they look for a place of their own. They want one nearby so Helen can help look after Ma, whose health is declining. They find a duplex about a mile away. It is there that I am born, another George, named for my father, but called Tony by my mother and hence by everyone except strangers and bureaucracies. My mother stays home with me, while my father immerses himself in his new job as a traveling salesman. For several years, days are bright.

One awful day in the spring of 1943, however, dark clouds appear. Flash, like so many others, is called to war. My mother and I return to Sherman Avenue. Now, decades later, I imaginatively return to that house.

On the night before he leaves for service, Flash stands in Ma's living room in what might have been a repeat of his first welcome to the old gray home. But now the mood is somber. Underneath the surface of casual conversation, anxiety swirls. It passes over me as I play on the floor, but I feel it today.

Flash, a drink in hand, takes George aside.

"Watch over the boy," he says, with an intensity that startles George. "You know I'm coming back from this. But until I do, Helen will really need your help. And you'll be the only man around for him. Do this for me, George."

I imagine George, a short time later, looking at me playing with my toy train. He must wonder what obligation he's assumed. As one man among women, George feels Flash's admonition has a special meaning. He is, after all, not just an uncle. He's a photographer, story-teller, and fisherman. For me, a boy soon to be three, he could be more—a magician perhaps, and great fun. Surely, he concludes with enthusiasm, he is ready to meet Flash's charge.

As I walked slowly along Sherman Avenue headed for my grandmother's house some sixty-five years later, I remembered the walk of my father and uncle on this street. It wasn't a real memory though, because their meeting took place before I was born. It's just that I heard George's story so often, my imagination made a memory of it, like a film with George and Flash at the bar. Their walking home shot from a lofty perch in the old elms above. Interior scenes of genial conversation in the living room and at dinner. The climactic closeup of my father holding my mother's arm and dramatically announcing his intentions. Her deep gaze.

CLOUDS, CREELS,
AND CAMERAS

In the weeks following my father's departure, George installed a small wading pool in which Jake and I could splash with our friends now that the weather was warm. But, I imagine, he thought he should do more.

He began by introducing me to cloud watching, a game he'd played by himself on youthful walks in the fields that bordered the town. He'd been fascinated with a kaleidoscope his father had shown him. He loved to watch the patterns drift in and out of view. So on special days, he looked to the clouds piling up on one another as though they were a white on blue kaleidoscope. A high level wind, unfelt below, moved them with stately grace from one pattern to another in which he tried to see pictures. At college and even after he'd started working, George sometimes looked to the skies, wondering if the clouds held some message for him. But if they did, their shifting, twisting transformations erased anything written there before he could decipher it.

There we'd be, George and I, lying on a grassy spot in the backyard, spectators to performances overhead. George would point out animals or fairy tale characters forming in the sky. But his cat might be my horse. Or a character from one of my books that seemed so clear to my uncle might stay hidden from me. And it wasn't long before I could find figures in the clouds that George had missed. He marveled at my discoveries. Who would have thought that a pirate ship floated above us? But as George learned long ago, the twisting assemblies in the sky made agreement on any particular cloud picture provisional at best. While this made watching engaging, it also made it frustrating. What we saw never lasted.

When autumn came, George introduced me to leaf jumping, for which I needed no training. Seeing me crowned with leaves and twigs, he felt some of the joy of those days when he himself rolled in leafy piles. He may well have taken secret pleasure in my mother's irritated reaction, so like Ma's, to the cleaning that followed our homecoming.

George kept his fisherman's collection of tied flies and old wicker creels in a downstairs den in Ma's house. The flies intrigued me. In their flat boxes, bright-colored and feathered, they seemed to be the miniature flags of a miniature army. But they were dangerous. When my uncle returned from fishing, I sometimes saw a fish or two in his creel, and once, one had a brightly feathered hook in its mouth. Uncle George warned me that sharp points hid under the plumage. He pressed the barb of a hook against my palm to emphasize the danger. I could almost feel it tearing my reddened skin. From then on, I never got too close to the flies for fear that one might somehow snag me.

The creels were much safer, and my uncle let me play with them. He had three or four woven from wicker, with leather straps holding the tops to the baskets and longer straps for carrying them. The wicker, which had been varnished, was smooth and shiny except in a few places where splintered pieces stuck out. When I lifted the top of a creel, it creaked slightly. The tops had secondary openings, little doors through which I could peer into the baskets. Uncle George told me that these let you see the fish inside, but kept them from jumping out. So when I played with these creels, I put several of my toy soldiers inside and peered in at them through the top. They were my prisoners, and I had to make sure that they couldn't escape.

At one end of the den was my uncle's darkroom, off limits to me. He did allow me to sit on the floor outside, where I looked at picture books while he worked. Sharp smells wafted from under the door, and sounds of sloshing liquids mingled with intermittent mumbling and singing. Sometimes he came out of his darkroom with nothing to show for his efforts. His black and white prints were either drying or "just no damn good" and consigned to the trash.

In time, he let me into the darkroom to watch him work with his enlarger and trays of developing solutions. I was excited watching the images form under the liquid. They swirled into being like formations in the clouds. As he deftly moved the paper around in the solutions, he urged me to guess what image would appear. Too soon, and I had no idea of what the picture would be. Too late, and I got no credit for guessing it. Once the images materialized, however, they remained fixed, unlike clouds.

I was the subject of many of my uncle's pictures. By the front door dressed in a sailor coat, the handle and part of a wagon visible at my side, poised to embark on a journey. Next to my strikingly handsome father, who is still in his uniform on the joyous day of his return from the war. Both of us dazed by the sudden change in our lives. Finally, with my parents, reaching across my shoulders to embrace each other—the three of us entwined, laughing in a record of a happy homecoming.

My father had been cast into a maelstrom of violence and slaughter, but he'd survived.

INSECT SONGS

During my reunion, I found time to explore my childhood neighborhoods. On one walk I passed the duplex apartment my parents rented before my father was called to war. It was now part of a florist shop. I continued to the house my parents bought after the war, a small split-level with three bedrooms above and a family room below the main floor. Except for an extension on the garage, it seemed little changed. The maple tree I'd planted with my father now had grand branches spreading over a large segment of the lawn. Standing there I suddenly remembered another contribution I made, a $100 war bond. One day my parents asked me if they could apply the cost of the bond to the cost of the new house. I hadn't known of the bond and hardly understood what it was, but I was very proud to contribute.

On weekends, when my father was at home, we some-times walked along one of the paths to the mountains, past the fields near our house. He taught me to listen to the singing of the insects hidden in the grass and trees. As a child, he'd walked with his father through the fields of a farm in Ohio. The old man had taught him to listen to their song.

I later learned that the music of the crickets came from the rubbing of their limbs, but that of the cicada came from special structures in their bodies. On the hillside trails, I would sometimes hear just one insect voice in solo. Only occasionally did the whole cacophonous song reverberate. Then a crescendo, harsh and insistent, would separate from the communal song. I would catch my breath and quiet myself in anticipation of some announcement. When that swell subsided, I relaxed. The message hadn't come; perhaps another day.

Now, looking past those fields toward the low mountains, I heard that chorus again. A song of sadness. I remembered how my father changed after his return from war. He was again a traveling salesman, but for a large silverware company. His territory, which he covered by car, extended across much of New England. He usually left on Monday morning and returned late in the week. This was his regular routine until I was in college.

My father was often very different in public than he was at home. Among outsiders, he returned to his college days, appearing as Flash, the hearty backslapper with the gift of gab. He was very popular with neighbors and attractive to strangers, as well. In bars, stores, and hotels, he made friends easily on his travels.

But at home, while glimpses of Flash could still be seen, a less congenial personality might suddenly show itself. A neighbor drops by late in the afternoon. My father offers him a drink. The two sit, exchanging gossip and stories, Flash on full display. When the neighbor departs, Flash, with best regards to the visitor's wife, his children, and even his dog, urges a quick return. As soon as the door closes, however, he grumbles about the incivility of someone who comes just before dinner and doesn't leave quickly. "What an ass!" he says.

He was also quick to criticize failings in my attitude or behavior. During his long absences, my mother necessarily made many decisions and accommodations without his counsel. I think he felt left out of my life. But I did not know how I should connect with my father, particularly when he would soon be gone again. Uncle George, too, found him difficult.

SLEDDING WITH GEORGE

We lived near what was then the edge of town, still only two miles from Sherman Avenue. It was a short distance from some wooded hills that encompassed the Sand Bank. During the last wartime winters, Uncle George took me sledding there. Most people approached the hills from the sandy side for which it had been named. Two slopes, about two blocks apart, rose to a forested ridge of pine trees and scrub bushes. Between them, near the center of the ridge, the ground sloped more steeply to create a large half-bowl. Down the left taper ran a trail, which served as a toboggan run. But daredevils—a group that included a few adults and almost every child older than seven—plunged on their sleds directly on the slopes closer to the center of the ridge. In the bowl, less adventurous parents and the youngest children on sleds or in wagons milled around. The bowl was also the place for snowball fights.

I often stood at the top of the gentler slope, sled at the ready, waiting for my uncle's urging from below to throw myself on and plow down the hill. At the bottom, George marveled at my speed and style. Then I happily trudged back up, dragging my sled behind. In the late afternoon, dusk settled in after a few runs, making the final descent even more dramatic.

Over the course of the next winter, when I was turning five, my uncle opened new vistas for me. He clambered up the hill to show me paths through the trees down the backside. Only older boys challenged these trails on sleds, sometimes returning with scrapes from failing to negotiate one of the sharp turns in the dim, snowy forest. Once, George abruptly and awkwardly seated himself on the sled and pushed off down the trail. His cries of elation, mixing with the rustling of branches, abruptly stopped as he pulled to a halt before a challenging drop off in the path. Huffing and dusted with snow, he hauled himself and the sled back up the trail to where I waited, laughing and applauding.

Then George took several steps down a path I hadn't noticed under the trees, one well worn with more gentle curves. Settling me on the sled and sternly warning me to look out, he sent me down with a push. I can still feel the thrill of that ride.

One sunny afternoon in the winter of 1947, when a big snow covered everything, George and Barbara stopped by our house to visit Helen. Matters concerning Ma and the house on Sherman Street were weighing on them. Although Ma seldom complained, it was becoming difficult to care for her. They needed Helen's help. With his fidgeting and only partly muffled coughing, George soon made it clear he wanted no part of such a conversation. So to be rid of him, my mother suggested he take me sledding, an assignment he gladly accepted.

We stood on top of the Sand Bank, again. George and I peered through the falling flakes at the trail that snaked down under the trees on the back side of the hill. As always, while I mounted the sled, George cautioned me about speeding and cornering. Then with a shout, he gave me a shove. Off I went under snow falling from the sky and sliding off branches. George heard my joyous shout, some crackling of pine boughs, and then silence. In a moment, my harsh cry reached him. He called out, but my only answer was another cry.

Almost strangled by fear, George started down the trail, grabbing branches to steady himself along the way. The path was dim under the snowy pines. But ahead, my crying was a sure guide. Snow got into his boots, and twigs scraped his face. He stepped awkwardly on a rock under a drift, and pain shot through his ankle. He soon found me near the trail, sitting on my sled. My forehead was bruised and bleeding, and my hand and wrist hung limply from my sleeve. At George's arrival, I stopped crying, but continued to shake until George awkwardly embraced me.

I had taken a curve too fast, left the track, and run into a tree. The bruise on my head didn't bother me much, although the swelling and a trickle of blood alarmed George. But my hand and wrist were somehow numb and sore at the same time. George ministered to my head with a handful of snow and steadied my wrist in my jacket, making a sort of sling with one of the pockets. Then, like two wounded warriors, we trudged back up the hill, the sled trailing behind. But George knew that no hero's welcome awaited us.

After their initial alarm, my mother and Barbara took charge of my care. They washed my face and daubed hydrogen peroxide on my forehead. They were sure the swelling would recede in a day or so, leaving only a bruise for a few days more. They were less certain about my arm and wrist. I was able to move my fingers, a sign they took that nothing was broken. But the pain and numbness in my wrist worried them. So they gently wrapped it in heavy gauze and called the doctor, who said it was likely a simple sprain.

Discomfited by their ministrations, George fled to the bathroom to tend to his own scrapes. When he returned, he encountered my father, who had just arrived from his weekly travel. Helen was saying that boys will be boys, that I would soon recover, no worse for wear. My father brushed her aside. He turned on George, demanding to know the circumstances of the accident, breaking off frequently to get confirmation from me, who for the first time felt somehow in the wrong.

"You've got to be careful! What were you thinking, son, going down the backside like that?" my father shouted.

Suddenly, banging his fist on the table, he lashed out, "Goddam you, George. Can't you do anything right? Couldn't you even look after the kid for an hour? Jesus Christ!! How could you be so stupid?"

The air was sucked from the room. George gasped, but couldn't breathe. He was suffocating. He bolted from the kitchen and stumbled to his car. He sat behind the wheel panting for several minutes before he finally drove off through the lightly falling snow. Helen pushed Flash into the living room, leaving Barbara to tend to me and wait for the doctor. And I tried to hold back more tears.

THE SECRET DRAWER

Over time, George recovered from my father's tongue-lashing, but he stopped by the house only when he knew Flash was traveling. Sometimes he brought new prints. Once or twice, a fish or two in a creel. When he had photographs, he spread them on the floor in our living room as he'd done back in his den.

One Thursday when I was ten, as he leaned back against a chest in our front room, Uncle George reminded me that it once sat in his bedroom at Sherman Avenue.

"It's got a secret drawer, you know. I used to hide some of my pictures in it," he said, pulling a pillow away to pat the underside of the piece.

I immediately saw that what appeared to be a skirt for the chest was in fact a shallow drawer. Playfully pushing him aside, I pulled it open. Inside were a few papers, some photographs, and what looked like old candy bars.

"What are these?" I asked, holding one of the bars out to George.

"K-rations," answered George, turning a bar over several times. "Food for the soldiers during the war. Like chocolate."

And pictures, but not by George. My father, standing with other soldiers amid shattered buildings in ruined streets. Another print showed him standing alone by a tank. Flash, a real War Hero.

"Look at these," I exclaimed, spreading the photographs for George to see.

But George was looking at several other, larger prints he'd lifted from the drawer.

"Oh, my God," he grimaced, and quickly slid them face down into one of his folders. "Ask your father about those," he said pointing to mine. He struggled up and lurched from the room, slamming the door behind him as he left the house. I was startled, but quickly returned to study my pictures.

Later that afternoon, when my father arrived, I rushed him with the pictures, spilling out questions about the war.

"Son," he said, "Put that stuff away. The real heroes are dead."

He patted me on the head, turned, and slowly left the room. So ended my first encounter with the War Hero.

I returned the pictures to the drawer. Later I approached my mother to tell her of my discovery. My excited questioning got another warning to leave the pictures alone. Obviously frustrated by my pestering, she insisted that my father wanted it that way. And, claiming something important to do, she abruptly left the room. The lure of the photographs remained strong. The next day, when my parents were out talking with neighbors, I slipped into the front room and quickly and quietly opened the secret drawer. It was empty.

So I was left to wonder about my father's time in the war. Occasionally my mother asked him about pains in his leg, which I learned were caused by still embedded shrapnel. But my father's slight limp seemed all that testified to his time in battle.

One afternoon, years later, I was cleaning my room, purging it of accumulated toys from earlier days. My father entered, and turning to greet him, I knocked my box of toy soldiers off a shelf. They fell to the floor, splayed as though casualties of battle. My father stood unmoving, staring down at the toyland carnage. He began shaking. In a voice raspy and cracking, almost unrecognizable, he croaked, "You could never know . . ." and stumbled from the room.

Again I was at a loss. I looked down on my scattered soldiers arrayed in their bright colors. I thought of the flies with hooks hidden under their feathers.

GEORGE FADES AWAY

George and Barbara continued to live with Ma, but despite our frequent visits to Sherman Avenue, I saw much less of my uncle than I had during the war. When I did find him at home, I headed to the den to play with the creels or see his latest pictures. When I outgrew toy soldiers, the creels lost their appeal. Still, there were stacks of his photographs on his desk, piled on a chair, or scattered on the floor. In them, I always found something engaging. Something to reconnect me with Uncle George.

At home when my parents talked about George, I began to recognize a certain tone in their conversation, one they used when they were exasperated with me. Even when my mother said she loved her brother dearly or my father declared what a smart guy he was, I sensed that they thought there was something wrong with him. I was beginning to learn that my uncle was "eccentric."

In time my parents' picture of my uncle became mine. There we'd be, a group of twelve-year olds with our basketball coach in an otherwise empty gym. Well, not quite. My uncle, in a rumpled blue suit with his tie arranged haphazardly, stood alone at the far end watching us play. Even in summer, he wore his overcoat or hung it over his arm. And indoors, he often wore his battered hat. In later years, he'd be by the baseball diamond or near the football field, dressed the same way, looking lost.

I usually met him after games, but George never had much to say. Later, when there were bigger crowds, he just faded away once play was over. Occasionally a teammate called attention to him, adding some comment about his appearance. When I was younger, I hadn't noticed his blotchy red face, his odd mustache, his dandruff, his big belly, his heavy breathing, all of which attracted the unkind notice of my friends. What bothered them now bothered me. I began to find my uncle not just an eccentric, but an embarrassment as well.

When Ma died a few years later, George started to drink heavily. On several occasions, my parents left on rescue missions to pick him up at some bar or to help him recover at home. Remarkably, even during his times of heavy drinking, George kept a part-time actuarial job. Perhaps his erratic behavior was seen as a manifestation of his widely noted eccentricity. Then, one of these rescue missions ended at the hospital. Not just because George was drunk, but because he was sick. Very sick, it turned out, although no one seemed to know the cause of his illness.

I visited my uncle a couple of days after his admission. He looked strange, wearing some kind of hair net and covered by a sheet pulled up to his chin. How different he sounded when he spoke. His voice, which had always been raspy, came even more hoarsely from a hollow deep within. He seemed less to speak his words than to expel them with contractions of his abdomen. The sheet over his big stomach lifted and fell raggedly.

While I stood at the foot of his bed, George whispered a few broken sentences, but mostly he drifted in and out of sleep. I found it hard to look at him. I knew he was dying. When I was sure he was sleeping, I moved closer. His face appeared quite clear. There was little of the redness, the blotches, the crusty patches that had for so long made him unattractive to so many. Instead, his skin looked almost untouched by age or the difficult life he'd led. He looked so different, it was hard to believe Uncle George lay before me. I remember wondering if I'd imagined the transformation.

George died five days after my sixteenth birthday, in 1956. On the way from the funeral to the cemetery, I finally asked my mother about his face. It turned out I hadn't imagined the change. She, too, had been startled by it. Her theory was that his skin problems "had gone inside" and somehow killed him. This didn't make sense to me, but I had no better explanation.

Years later, I came no closer to understanding what had happened. But whenever I saw an old picture of George with the ravaged face of the lonely eccentric, the unmarked countenance of my uncle's last days hovered over it. I again wondered about the transformation. How had I got George as an uncle in the first place—and how, even before the hospital, had I lost him? Finally, I thought of my uncle as a cloud himself. In his hospital bed, his old burdensome complexion dissolved, and his new clear features appeared. For a brief time, he displayed to his nephew, his sister—and Flash—a truer manifestation of his inner self. Then, like a cloud, he slowly turned and faded away.

FORTITUDE

Three years before George died, Ma came to live with us. She would stay in our third bedroom, and we would care for her.

My father and uncle carried her awkwardly up the stairs to her new room. Her chair, radio, some photographs, and a few other possessions followed. My mother served her dinner in her room and helped her prepare for bed. On that first night, Ma was able to walk from her chair to the bathroom and on to bed. But it wasn't long before that trek proved too much.

When my father left on his sales trips, care for Ma fell almost wholly to my mother. She got some support from Barbara and George, who made regular visits. But in those days, my notion of responsibility was limited.

So while I was happy to visit Ma and gossip with her, I contributed little else to her care.

Some months after Ma's arrival, the family decided to sell the house on Sherman Avenue. Her departure had set my aunt and uncle adrift. With modest expectations, they moved to separate apartments in the neighborhood, but soon, their lives began to deteriorate. George drank heavily and started the downward spiral that three years later ended in a hospital bed. Barbara, too, began to drink to excess. Her decline stretched over five or six years. Then my parents began repeating the late-night runs they had made trying to salvage George. Too often Barbara had to call in sick while she recovered. She lost several jobs.

After a months-long stay in a local treatment center, Barbara returned. For a time, she found office work, which she did well. Colleagues found her capable, sweet, and kind. But then another late-night call. A repeat performance. So she returned to treatment. When that sojourn was followed by another failure, it was apparent that Barbara couldn't live in the everyday world. My mother settled her in a state hospital for treatment. Until her death, Barbara lived and worked at the hospital. When I saw her again, twenty years later, she was calm and gentle with an easy sense of humor, having somehow pacified the forces that had drawn her into darkness.

At our home, Ma slowly declined. Now, each night, my mother roused herself from sleep to help her use a bedpan and to turn her in bed. In this, she got no help from me, nor did she ask for it. And even when my father was home, I think he was exempted from duty. So while Ma remained kind and appreciative for her care, she placed a heavy burden on my mother.

It was torturous for them. Should they move Ma to a nursing home? For my father, the answer was yes. While my mother agreed in principle, she was deeply worried by stories of old people who died when they were sent to such facilities. My father countered that these people were already close to dying. That's why they were in nursing homes. But still my mother feared it was rejection and abandonment that killed them. Finally, after weeks of discussion, they moved Ma to a nursing home several miles away. She died there a month later.

Ma and George were dead, and Barbara was safely in treatment, so the weight on my mother lightened. But, of course, not fully. My father still spent many days on the road, and for much of the time, she was a single parent as she had been during the war. Then George and Barbara shared care of me, giving her breaks and even chances for some part-time work. Now my long days at school offered her time for her own interests and activities.

I have little recollection of what she did for herself. I do remember that she became my greatest sports fan. She learned baseball, football, and basketball lingo and strategy. She made herself a very knowledgeable observer and critic. On Sunday afternoons, when I was home during my college years, I'd hear my parents debating the intricacies of professional football. She held up her end of the conversation. My father attended weekend football, basketball, and baseball games, but at mid-week games, my mother was my expert rooting section.

During my high school summers, she made sure I was amply fortified for my work. I dug ditches for the city, did road repair for the county, and shoveled rock, wood chips, and sulfur at a paper mill. To each job, I toted a metal lunch box containing two sandwiches—thick slices of bologna or liverwurst slathered with mustard on white bread—some cookies, and a quart of milk. The lunch of champions.

Not only did she master sports and lunches, she became a very competent handyman. She painted woodwork and hung wallpaper. She refinished some of Ma's furniture, old pieces that emerged from years of dust and grime to stand beautifully in our small house. Some handed down from Nantucket, where my mother's ancestors first settled. One of these pieces, a small pine secretary, houses my collection of Greek books.

When snow came during weekdays, my mother shoveled our walk and driveway with my assistance. I suppose she felt I was unlikely to damage myself or our property with a shovel. Eventually, the job became all mine. In summer, she mowed our lawn until she was sure I was up to the task. Even after assigning the job to me, she planted, weeded, and trimmed in the yard. None of this seemed unusual to me. She was always industrious. Although she might grumble briefly about how much she had to do, she never complained for long about the demands on her.

When they were in their sixties, my parents took a trip to Ireland. My father for long had professed a great love for the "Old Sod," a place he had never visited. He culled from his mother's records some markers of places from which his ancestors had come on their migration to the United States. On the map he even found a town with our name. So off they went on what they later reported was a wonderful trip. But their venture had surreptitiously exacted an additional price from my mother, one that she was to pay for over the rest of her life.

She contracted a form of pneumonia that proved resistant to the normal intervention of antibiotics. Her doctor prescribed steroids, and while they suppressed her symptoms, they brought notable side effects. Her skin thinned, and as a consequence, bruised and even tore easily. So for years, her arms were marked with splotches of dull purple and Band-Aids. When she bumped into something which added another mark, I might hear her grumble, but never complain. The memories she recounted of the trip only included the good times they'd had.

As I was later to see more clearly, my mother met her life day by day. She seldom, if ever, agonized about her circumstances—at least not in my presence. She simply and steadfastly did what life called upon her to do, and she did it often with much good humor and grace. Unlike my father when he was Flash, she didn't have a gravitational force that attracted the quick notice of others. In time, however, those who knew her recognized her qualities. Flash had been right all those years ago.

WAR STORIES

Before I left for college, my father's company promoted him to a new a job in New York City. I helped my parents pack for their move to Connecticut. In the concealed drawer of the old chest, I again found a couple of the photographs I'd seen some years before. And now with them, five black rectangular boxes stamped with gold letters: Purple Heart, Silver Star, Bronze Star, another Silver Star and finally, Distinguished Service Cross. Each held a medal attached to a colored ribbon. The Silver Stars gleamed against the black velvet interior of their boxes. The Purple Heart, enamel with gold trim, also shone. The Bronze Star and the Distinguished Service Cross, however, sat dully in their cases. I understood the meaning of the Purple Heart: my father had been wounded. The yellowed typewritten papers told me about the others. From them I learned for the first time of my father's "gallantry," "courage," and "extreme heroism." The citations laconically recounted incredible actions and seemingly impossible deeds for which he had been honored.

He had received the Distinguished Service Cross, the second-highest decoration that can be awarded to a member of the U.S. Army, for "extraordinary heroism" during fighting in eastern France in the months following the Normandy invasion. Even today, I marvel reading these terse accounts of his exploits, the first stories of my father's life in war. Although badly wounded, he had inflicted "severe casualties" on the enemy. He had single-handedly captured more than thirty German soldiers. He had escaped from a German prison. On that day of discovery so long ago, excited by these accounts of my father's prowess and bravery, I gave but a quick look at the photographs. They were snapshots showing him with other soldiers amid shattered buildings in ruined streets. One, which well matched my father of the citations, showed him standing alone by a tank. The citations, which I reread with growing excitement and pride, mattered most. Again, my father was a War Hero.

I wanted to quiz him about his experiences, to marvel at his tales of valor, and to ask why he had hidden his medals. "Son," he said, "put those back where you found them. I said before, the real heroes didn't come back. They're dead. I'm here with you and your mother. That's enough." So ended my second encounter with my father, the War Hero.

More than seventy years ago, he had been cast into that chaos of violence and slaughter. Many of his comrades died; several times he was wounded; he killed; he survived having repeatedly distinguished himself as a brave and resourceful soldier. He could have come home cloaked in fame, but for the rest of his life, he deflected questions about combat experiences. During fifty years, he gave me only three brief glimpses into his life in battle, three brief "war stories."

The first: He had been in the initial wave of soldiers to land on the beaches of Normandy. The Germans had laid large rolls of barbed wire just feet from the surf to impede the advance of the invaders. Raked by machine gun fire, soldiers wading out of the water had to crawl over this wire to gain a foothold on the beach. "If I hadn't been an officer," he said, "I'd be dead. I was moving men forward from the landing craft. The first threw themselves on the wire, clawing to get across. The machine guns got most of them. We crawled over their backs." With tears in his eyes, he said quietly, "All I went through with those men . . . I loved them."

The second: He had been wounded when German fire blew him out of a vehicle. He lay on the ground while the battle raged around him. "I carried a pistol in my vest," he said, "but my arm was pinned down, and I couldn't get to it. I was lucky. If I'd started shooting, the Germans would've killed me. When the fighting stopped, they found me and took me prisoner." Fragments of metal still embedded in his leg reminded him of that day his life hung so precariously in the balance.

The third: He had been in a barn in the German countryside where a hidden enemy soldier was trying to kill him. "I crept around some hay bales and got behind him," he said. "I killed him. I turned his body over . . . he was just a kid. Maybe fifteen. That was the war," he concluded and walked slowly away.

What did these stories mean? How could I understand them? Over the years, I often pondered them, particularly the chilling encounter with the boy in the barn. In time, like my father's first walk with my uncle, my imagination slowly wove my skeins of memory into a story. Seeing is believing. Believing is seeing. I felt I had been with him at that barn.

THE BOY IN THE BARN

L ate in an autumn afternoon in 1944, the sun descends slowly over the countryside in eastern
France. An impressionist painter, it tints the undersides
of clouds in their stately procession. It dapples the small
farm below in soft pastels, blurring the rooflines of a
house and a barn. It whitens the roughly rectangular
field that runs gently downhill from the buildings to a
stand of trees. The structures mark the upper corners
of its canvas. A small creek marks one side, glinting as
it meanders through patches of brambles. Opposite, a
fence of darkened split logs defines the other. Several
clumps of trees, their leaves beginning to yellow, form a
ragged lower edge.

In imagination, I drift above the field. I see the
painting as a *pentimento*, a recasting that reveals traces

of earlier work. The sun-whitened grass testifies to the passage of tanks and machine guns, the devastation of bombs, mortars and grenades. The corpses are gone and the battered survivors have moved on. But some splintered branches and a few deep gouges recall the fiery passing when the field was a plot in Hell. Perhaps the sun repents that awful picture and now covers it with beauty.

But death returns to the field. Sunlight spills into a stand of trees at the end of the field. Five men are gathered there. The light streaks their faces, their helmets, and their worn uniforms. It ripples on the metal of their rifles as it does on the surface of the slow creek.

Then, three move along the trees to the left and cross behind the wooden fence. In its modest cover, they move slowly toward the farmhouse. The other two exit the trees to the right. Once through the brambles, they begin an approach to the barn, wading in the ankle deep water of the stream. Its low bank offers a bit of protection.

When he reaches the water, the first of the two stands momentarily motionless, listening. At first he hears nothing. But he knows an insect chorus is singing. He has heard it in Ohio. In this field near the German border, far from home, the chorus again swells. He listens. Does it sing his coming death?

Months before, in the maelstrom on the beach, too many of his men had died. Impaled on barbed wire and raked by German machine guns, their bodies made a gruesome bridge which he and his comrades had scrambled across.

Although the Germans were in retreat, isolated

groups stayed behind to wreak havoc on the unwary. Just a week ago, when victory seemed assured, he'd lost one of his men to sniper fire. In the earlier drive across France, he himself had been blown from a vehicle, wounded, and taken prisoner. Only his harrowing escape from the German prison camp had returned him to his men. Now he knows that neither bravery nor moral worth assures anyone's survival. A blend of heroism, madness, and ferocity now pushes him on. At times, he is indifferent to fear, pain, and even the prospect of oblivion.

He studies the field and farm buildings carefully. A bitter darkness can descend swiftly on even the most beautiful scene. But seeing nothing amiss, he steps into the stream and starts slowly toward the barn, while the tremulous song of insects floats in the air.

I imagine him wading step by step toward the barn against the slow-moving water. Some larger clumps of brambles and a few scrubby bushes provide him refuge. Still, he moves fitfully from one cover to another, waiting, watching, and listening before striking out for the next. His comrade follows behind, replacing him in one hiding spot after another as he moves forward. Near the barn, there are fewer brambles and bushes. An old wagon some twenty yards up from the creek offers a last protection. Missing a wheel, it tilts obliquely. Like a crab, he scuttles through the grass from the creek to the backside of the wagon. He can see the barn door. He motions to his companion who wriggles up to him following his trail, still pressed in the grass. They lie still, and he listens. The insects sing.

Behind the wagon, using only gestures, the two plan

their final approach to the barn, which squats some twenty yards ahead. Rusted tools are stacked against its facing side, which shows two windows, one boarded, one slightly open. They can't see the back of the barn or its other sides.

His companion stirs and crawls toward the front of the cart, seeking a better view of the long side of the barn, then raises his arm to signal an advance. The air splits as a bullet hisses through it to rip open his raised shoulder. He screams and falls head first behind a wagon wheel. A red blossom spreading on the back of his shirt confirms the passage of metal through flesh.

Seizing the wounded man's ankles, my father drags him to a less exposed position. He does his best to staunch the bleeding and then turns to face the threat from the barn. Across the field, his other men have disappeared. Under cover after the shot. The air is still.

The attic door would obscure the shooter's view of the back of the wagon. The shot had come from the right side. So that left path is better, but still harrowing. A crouching zigzag of twenty yards, which, if he survives, will bring him to the side of the door. A door to death? Despite a thumping heart, he scrambles across the dirt yard to the barn.

Another bullet slices the air and throws up pebbles a few feet from his legs. The shot came from above. So at the barn, he stands and presses his back flat against the siding to offer the smallest target. He listens. The insects, silenced by the shots, resume their singing. But he hears nothing else.

He inches sideways to the door and slips into the barn through the open frame. He crouches, sheltered by the side of a stall. The building is divided into several sections. One is filled with hay. Another with piles of logs and cut branches. And there are some farm implements in one corner. A wooden stair rises to the attic. From his hiding place, he can see no more. He hears no one. He waits watching dust motes dance in the light that spreads several paths through the space. And he listens.

Time stops in this one moment of life or death.

Then he notices a small wrench hanging from a nail at the edge of the stall. Slowly, scarcely breathing, he carefully lifts it. Without looking, he throws it toward the back of the barn. It clangs off some metal. And immediately the rifle fires again, its bullet ricocheting off metal as well. It has announced its position. He sees a crouching figure scrambling for the hay bin. One shot of his own, then another, and their combat abruptly ends. He is the victor. His enemy lies unmoving, sprawled face down on the sun-splattered floor. A pool of bright blood is already forming under his neck. The rifle lies nearby.

He calls to his men. From the back of the barn, they report all clear on their side. Hold fire.

With his own rifle ready, he cautiously approaches the body, which is slight and wears a shabby German uniform. With his foot, he prods it, confirming that his enemy is dead. He rolls him onto his back. The lifeless eyes of a young boy, certainly no older than fifteen, stare up at him.

His men burst into the back of the barn. They scan the barn again, and then rush to him. He hasn't moved. He stands, transfixed by that face. One of his men shakes his arm, and urges him away. He shakes his head as though coming out of a trance. Then he slowly leads the men to their wounded comrade, who lies outside behind the wagon.

He looks back at the boy, who lies impossibly still. His blood spreads slowly on the barn floor. The light from the setting sun grows dim. Six months later, the man is back home, surrounded by family and friends. He fought. He was wounded. He killed. He survived. He rose in rank. But medals and citations that testify to his gallantry and heroism are hidden away.

In a photograph of a joyous homecoming he exudes happiness. Now I know that the image is no *pentimento*. The camera hasn't detected the traces of other images that lie beneath. They are too deeply hidden: the corpse-covered barbed wire, the savaged bodies, blood and spattered brains, a dead boy on a barn floor. Nor can it see the scars left on his heart. It can't detect the sorrow of knowing that even a great hero can't save his beloved comrades from fate. And it can't hear the incessant threnody that echoes in his head, the message that is delivered every day.

STORIES IN AN
OLD LANGUAGE

> The Greeks, generally speaking, were endowed with spiritual force that allowed them to avoid self-deception. The rewards of this were great; they discovered how to achieve in all their acts the greatest lucidity, purity, and simplicity.
> —*Simone Weil*

A man set plates spinning atop a row of poles. He hustles back and forth from one pole to another, giving each just enough spin to keep its plate from falling. But as he attends to one plate, others teeter precariously. Too much attention to one means disaster for others. Not enough means that this one will fall. This vaudeville performer's success depends on giving to each pole just enough attention to keep its plate aloft. As he goes, an assistant adds a new pole and plate, demanding even more speed from him. The number of poles quickly becomes so great that he has to conduct his act on the dead run.

In my life, I was going from email to cell phone to computer screen, keeping each assignment or project going with a quick spin or fast adjustment. As technology increased the number of these poles, the attention I could devote to each diminished. I was giving to each just enough and often, no more. In particular, I found myself paying less and less attention to the past, caught up as I was with the rush of the future.

I needed to retire my own vaudeville act, or at least to revamp my performance. So now, beside the chair in which I do much of my writing, there is a small bookcase with several rows of colorfully covered books, orange, blue, and green. They're classics texts, epics and plays in ancient Greek. It was the hectic pace of my life that put them there several years after my father's death.

In these books, as Virginia Woolf said, we encounter original human beings, decided, ruthless, and direct, before their emotions have been worn to uniformity. With less eloquence, I would have expressed the same sentiments. I had read many of these works in translation, but some of their meaning seemed to lie on the far side of language. I had given occasional thought to learning Greek. I did not wish for the impossible—to become a Greek of Euripides' time—but rather by learning the language I would come closer to the heart of his work and that of others. A couple of beginning efforts sputtered and faded out.

Now I had another reason to study ancient Greek—to counterbalance my invigorating, but unsettling, vaudeville act. Not only were Greek tragedies and epics engaging, they were stable and permanent, unchanged for more than two thousand years. Of course, each of these works has a history. What I took to be its fixity emerged from the sometimes conflicting efforts of scholars to arrive at a definite text. This scholarship was, however, peripheral to my interests. I was not interested in new releases or updates of the texts. Rather than keeping up with the epics and plays, I would have to work my way into them. They would stay put while I explored them. What would change would be my understanding.

My original interest in Greek was to know it well enough to read Homer, Aeschylus, Sophocles, and Euripides in their language. At the time, I didn't foresee how much from ancient times would find a way into my life, particularly in my understanding of what happened to my father in combat.

Think of learning any complex subject in the rush of today's life. You would need to put aside the pole-spinning of the digital age. Patience and prolonged involvement with your subject would be essential. You might find conventional perspectives a hindrance and need to adopt new ones. Understanding would likely come from repeated returns to your subject, from frequent revisions to what you had long assumed you knew. But the return on this investment might be great, as it was for me when I turned repeatedly to the complex subject of the past. Much of what I read, although written millennia ago, proved strikingly relevant to that undertaking. As I struggled to learn ancient Greek, I found new meaning in my father's medals.

I was an optimist, certain I'd soon be reading the work of the ancient tragedians with ease. Despite seven or eight years of somewhat haphazard study, however, the fluency I anticipated has yet to come. Sometimes I read whole segments of a work easily, but just as often, I labor to understand a few lines. Still, despite some significant diversions, I keep at my study with constancy that surprises me. What is there about the language, the plays—what is there about me—that keeps me engaged with ancient Greek?

The Greek language itself with its complex grammar and seemingly endless vocabulary was my primary hurdle. The tradition that for centuries has governed the teaching of ancient Greek meets this challenge with patient, long-term involvement with the language. This seems to have worked well, given time and competent teachers. Today, it is more difficult to engage in this traditional approach, because there are fewer students and fewer courses. But the obstacles to understanding Greek lie not only in its complex forms and convoluted syntax, but also in a separation of nature and spirit between us and the Greeks of ancient times. In an essay entitled "On Not Knowing Greek," Virginia Woolf said the meaning of a passage could hover "just on the far side of language." Yet she acknowledged that despite the labor and difficulty involved, we are drawn back again and again to the Greeks.

I could easily read the terse accounts of my father's heroics. I could recall his three brief war stories. But I was separated from the world of which they spoke. Behind the words, I felt meaning, as yet unrecovered, lay waiting. Who had my father been when he was the War Hero? My encounters with ancient Greek helped me answer this question.

I began my Greek study in the introductory class at Rice University as one of about fifteen students. I was what my mother would have called an odd duck—a university vice president among students mostly in their teens. Only a few of those students and I stayed into the second year, where we confronted texts of Plato, modestly abridged. Were we to teach swimming the way I was taught Greek, we might give children a couple of talks on hydrodynamics and then throw them into the water. For swimming, floundering about might prove effective, but keeping afloat in Greek is a different matter. In the few other classes I took, enrollment seldom exceeded a handful of students, some like me repeating classes when the texts changed. It was a good time, with good teachers, small classes, and great material. But too soon, I was on my own, motivated by stories of others who had taught themselves Greek and aided occasionally by faculty colleagues. Then, too, there were the resources of the Internet.

There are many traditional resources for someone studying Greek outside the classroom. Texts, commentaries, and translations are readily available. Good dictionaries and even some lexicons are at hand. The Information Age has brought new online aids. The most notable is the collection of classical texts in the Perseus Project. This remarkable repository contains all the texts I wanted to read, and a great many more, each linked through hypertext in a way that makes reading straightforward. With a page of the Greek text on my laptop, I can click on any word and jump to a comprehensive list of its possible forms and meanings. From any of these links, I can call up a brief or expanded dictionary entry for the root word, or with equal ease I can get an English translation of the text I am reading. By doing away with the need to puzzle out forms, rummage through the dictionary, and ponder meanings, Perseus offers an "efficient" approach to these classics, quite in keeping with the accelerated pace of modern life. Resources like this bolster our enthusiasm for cyberspace. But they can promote the learning just-enough-just-in-time, which may mean little learning at all.

At first, I added Greek to my life as another pole to spin. Despite my intentions to follow a traditional path of study, I found myself giving that pole just-enough-just-in-time attention to keep it upright. How else could I explain those repeated encounters with words whose meanings continued to lie just outside my grasp? It was because, too often, on meeting one of them, I had gotten just enough of its meaning to let me move on with my translation. I had learned just enough to get to the next speech or the next ode, but not enough for my larger ambition of knowing Greek.

Self-discipline, of course, could have alleviated this problem, but the temptation to learn just enough, to press ahead, to get going, was strong when novelty lay a click away. David Brooks says, "It's like you're circulating within an infinite throng with instant access to people you'd almost never meet in real life . . . You live in a state of perpetual anticipation because the next social encounter is just a second away." Hyperlink, email, cell phone: all called for immediate attention, each promising something more interesting or engaging, stirring restlessness and impatience for the new.

Yet my intention had been to know Greek in the older, more rigorous sense, an aim that went beyond accessing dictionary entries and translations from a web page. An occasional foray into the dictionary would be acceptable, but less to learn the basic meanings of a word than to check on nuance or connotation. Even those few people who might be said to know Greek, I suspect, keep a dictionary close at hand. When I originally pictured myself knowing Greek, I did not envision myself as an information retrieval specialist.

I began to think about memory in much the same way. With the artifacts from the shoebox, the photographs, my father's citations and medals, I could cobble quick, loosely knit stories about people and events. This meant writing. But often those constructions seemed facades behind which deeper understanding lay—understanding that would emerge only from patient, repeated exploration and invention.

Early in *Hippolytus*, the chorus recalls a rumor of Phaedra's puzzling illness. The story came first from women washing at a rock that was said to drip water from the river that circles the world. In the lines the women chant, Euripides makes the rock seem as far off and strange as Greek itself seemed to me. Were such a rock to exist today, I could "google" it to retrieve its longitude and latitude, something about its geology, even a picture. But knowing about the rock is not the same as knowing it. For that, I would have to go to the rock, walk around it, feel it, explore its nooks and crannies.

In the same way, I know the facts—when, where, the photographer—associated with the picture of Flash and Helen, arms together, laughing in his happy homecoming. But repeated considerations—reconsiderations—of that picture have brought me to a deeper understanding of its meaning.

There are, then, two ways I have thought about to approach Greek—one driven by an itch for speed and novelty, the other shaped by patience and care. If I am ever to know Greek, I must follow the older way, slowing myself down when I take up *Hippolytus*. There my approach to Greek is accretive, in distinction to much of my work, in which the new rapidly pushes aside the old. To learn Greek, I gradually add thin layers of understanding to previous ones. A colleague recently said she gains new insights even on her tenth reading of certain novels. The Greek tragedies and epics are like that for me; they repay repeated visits, not because they are new releases, but because with my slowly improving Greek, I am getting closer to them.

The same tension exists in visits to the past. One way favors the quick retrieval of facts. Remembrance becomes one of the tasks to be juggled among the other demands of the rush of the present. The other way demands a return of at least part of life to an older way of learning and contemplation. Even with the addition of electronic collections of traditional resources, learning Greek is still hard; it takes hours of study, time that might otherwise be devoted to keeping up with the rush of contemporary life. For me, however, effort has been worthwhile, for although I have far to go to know Greek, the great tragedies are now even greater than I had expected when I set out. Despite the millennia that stand between us and the ancient Greeks, their world need not remain alien to us. The authors of that time come to meet us once we accommodate the oddness of syntax and expression of their language. We find their concerns are often ours and hear echoes of their stories sounding through our lives.

In reading her essay "A Sketch of the Past," I felt Virginia Woolf might have been speaking for me when she said,

> The past only comes back when the present runs
> so smoothly that it is like the sliding surface
> of a deep river. Then one sees through the sur-
> face to the depths. In those moments I find one
> of my greatest satisfactions, not that I am think-
> ing of the past; but that it is then that I am liv-
> ing most fully in the present . . . But to feel the
> present sliding over the depths of the past, peace
> is necessary.

THE GREEK HERO

In Homer, I found a poet who across almost three millennia says much to help me understand my father, the War Hero. Now I imagine him in the company of the great warriors who fought beneath the walls of Troy. Each of his citations, other than its mention of modern weapons and technology, reads like what Homer calls an ἀριστεία, a combat that reveals the prowess of a great warrior. At the end of the twentieth book, when Achilles has finally joined the battle with the Trojans, Homer offers a description of the hero in combat. While I have much more to learn about Homer's language, my translation reveals his vivid simile:

> As a god-kindled fire will rage through the depth
> of hollows of a parched mountain and the deep

forest will blaze as the wind drives the fire to
every part, so Achilles dashed everywhere like
a wild god, trampling the men he killed, and
the earth was blackened with blood. [Book XX:
490–494]

Earlier in the text Homer says that Hector in a rout
of the Greeks was like a hunting dog that seizes on a
wild boar or a lion after a chase. And Patroclus, dear
companion to Achilles, hurled himself upon the Trojans three times, with wild yells in his throat. Each time
he killed nine men. But on the fourth, the end of life
loomed up for him. The language of my father's citations
is less poetic, but in it, the actions of a great warrior are
unmistakable—as are the frightful risks he faces.

His citation for the Distinguished Service Cross recounts how he

> . . . personally took command of a leaderless
> rifle platoon and led it against the enemy in the
> face of heavy machine gun, small arms, artillery
> and mortar fire . . . in the ensuing fight person-
> ally manned a machine gun mounted on a truck
> inflicting severe casualties on the enemy and pin-
> ning them down so that his greatly outnumbered
> patrol could withdraw to report the valuable
> information obtained. He then took a position in
> the lead vehicle of a tank column . . . and suffered
> a multiple fracture of one arm and severe concus-
> sion when his vehicle was knocked out by enemy
> fire. Refusing to be evacuated he proceeded by
> vehicle to locate four members of one of his mor-
> tar squads left behind in an exposed position

when their platoon was forced to withdraw. He proceeded on foot when the driver of his truck was killed and located the men. By pinning the enemy down with his submachine gun fire, he was able to safely lead his men out of danger.

Greatly outnumbered, my father went forth like a Homeric hero to engage the enemy. Wounded, he repeatedly threw himself at them and at death. And in the end, he triumphed. Had he been at Troy, great fame would have been his. Instead, in a half-hidden drawer, a few medals and some papers were the sole testaments to his prowess.

After ten years of war and ten more of an eventful voyage home, Odysseus arrives at Ithaca, where Athena disguises him as a wretched beggar so he can safely reconnoiter the situation in his house, so long occupied by his wife's suitors. With her magic wand, Athena shrivels his skin, makes his hair fall out, and dims his bright eyes. Odysseus becomes a hero secreted within an old man's wrinkled hide. But when he has completed his reconnaissance, the goddess touches him with her golden wand to reveal the mighty father to his awe-struck son.

When my father returned from war, he had no need to get the lay of the land. He was warmly welcomed, yet he donned a disguise. No goddess remade his appearance. He clothed himself in reticence, hiding the hero he had been. From the day I found his medals, I wanted my father to reveal himself fully. But to the end of his life, no goddess extended a magic wand to cast his disguise aside. Over the years, whenever I tried to get him to talk about his wartime experiences, he would only repeat one of the stories he had told me: his landing at Normandy and the deaths of the men he loved; his capture by the enemy; his killing of the German youth in the barn.

As I read Homer, slowly those stories merged with the poet's. In the battle that surges back and forth before the walls of Troy and the sea, nothing is certain. A chance arrow, a misstep, a stumbling horse, each can bring sudden doom on even the bravest. Heroism may gain renown, but it affords no salvation, not even for godlike Achilles. Fate and the changing rhythm of battle, not moral worth or even fighting skill, determine the victors and the vanquished, who will live a while more and who will die.

Homer is unsparing in his depiction of death. Spearheads split brains and disgorge their contents; teeth and eyes are dashed out, blood pours from mouths, nostrils, and wounds. Heroes quake in the face of death's enveloping black cloud. When Hector challenges the Greeks to send forth a champion to meet him in single combat, they huddle in silence and abject fear. Only when Ajax is chosen by lot to meet Hector's challenge, when each of the other Greeks knows he will not be the one to die, does sickening dread leave them. Now fear settles instead on the Trojans when they see the huge Ajax advancing with his great spear. Not even Hector himself is spared the terror that has descended on his comrades. His knees tremble and his heart thumps. But Homer allows no retreat; Hector has committed himself. He must put his life into the hands of fate.

Like Hector, my father may have felt cold fear come upon him. Yet, he moved steadfastly forward.

In moments of great peril, the heroes of the *Iliad* seem to become indifferent to fear, pain, and even the prospect of oblivion. Rachel Bespaloff identifies the agent of this transformation as a pervasive force, which "reveals itself in a kind of supreme leap, a murderous lightning stroke, in which calculation, chance, and power seem to fuse in a single element to defy man's fate." Homer shows that the force, which mixes heroism, madness, and ferocity, arises in the moment of trial. A warrior possessed by it can go berserk like Achilles, who, having killed Hector, abuses his corpse for days until Zeus sends Thetis, Achilles' mother, to tell him to accept Priam's gifts. These days, we would likely say that Achilles was in the grip of post-traumatic stress syndrome. Could it be that in combat, my father was not my father at all, but a being transformed by this force, a being outside any life I could know? If so, over the years, I saw few vestiges of the emotions that urged him forward in the face of death when he achieved his ἀριστεία.

Homer also tells us this force emerges only when wishful thinking, self-pity, self-deception, and even the consoling prospect of immortality are put aside. The gods hold sway over the lives of the warriors, willfully manipulating them to satisfy their own whims and ambitions. Greater fighters may be thwarted and lesser ones protected. The intervention of the gods can reverse fate, granting life or delivering doom in an instant. Through Apollo's intervention, Hector escapes death in his duel with Ajax, but later, confronting Achilles, he is doomed by doings on Olympus. Zeus places icons of Achilles and Hector on his golden scales, and

Hector's sinks toward the gloom. Apollo abandons him, Athena betrays him, and Hector must face death alone. Despite his bitter betrayal by the goddess, Hector turns with clear eyes to face Achilles and death. A Trojan ally, Sarpedon, looks at the perils of war with the same steady gaze. Now that a thousand shapes of death, which no man can escape, loom up, he says we must steel ourselves to attack. I believe the same clarity of vision steadied my father when he so often faced the prospect of death.

Our fates are no longer balanced on Zeus's golden scales. Still, a host of lesser gods—biological, social, political, emotional—tug at us, some with an insidious, grave intent. We may think Homer's gods vain, insensitive, manipulative, and petty, but the gods of war who thrust my father into battle were no more fair, no more just than those Olympians. Had he not been an officer at Normandy, had he been able to reach his revolver, had the German boy crept behind him in the barn, my father would likely have died. He was like Homer's heroes who, despite their prayers and sacrifices, cannot deflect fate. The poet teaches, however, that in that awful moment the hero can free himself from the grip of fear and bravely meet the lot the gods have assigned him.

Homer also teaches a sad truth that echoes in my father's stories. The greatest of heroes cannot save their beloved comrades from inexorable fate. Heartbroken and raging, Achilles cries inconsolably for Patroclus, who, wearing Achilles' armor, was killed by Hector. Years after the sack of Troy, moved by song of a Phaeacian harper, Odysseus sheds molten tears for the fallen Greeks. My father could never reconcile himself to the deaths of his comrades. His tears over my scattered toy soldiers marked an inexpressible sorrow, for which all his medals could not recompense him.

In the last book of the *Iliad*, Homer describes the meeting of Priam, Hector's father, and Achilles, his son's killer. Priam is begging for the return of his son's body. He humbles himself, lifting his lips to the hand of the fearsome warrior. Achilles is stirred by grief for his own father, who will soon mourn him as Priam does Hector, and for Patroclus. Together, the two men weep. Then Achilles draws Priam to his feet, saying: "We'll probe our wounds no more but let them rest, though grief lies heavy on us. Tears heal nothing, drying so stiff and cold. This is the way the gods ordained the destiny of men, to bear such burdens in our lives, while they feel no affliction."

During the Vietnam War, when I was of draft age, my worst fear of combat was not that I would die, but that I would prove a coward. So for some years, there was no talk of medals, but with the waning of that war, my anxiety ebbed. Seven years ago, however, my unease returned, ushered in by a doctor's report of an abnormality in my blood. The specialist who identified the problem as acute myeloblastic leukemia ran briskly through some numbers. The one that stood out was my chance of survival, twenty to thirty percent at best. I had been healthy and busy; now death loomed.

There was, however, little time to dwell on my prospects. Two days later, I entered the hospital to begin my first round of chemotherapy, which, including the time for my immune system to recover, kept me there for about a month. During my stay, I often thought about how my father had behaved in the face of death. And I read Homer, who has much to say about such confrontations. First I took up the *Iliad*, then inclined to the *Odyssey*, I suspect because it promised an ultimately successful homecoming. Since then, I have undergone much chemotherapy and two stem cell transplants, because leukemia, which for some months had seemed defeated, made a bitter return. Now I, too, am in the grip of fate. Each decision to choose or forego a treatment is fraught with uncertainty; even doctors seem unable or unwilling to argue for one or the other.

My father's time in combat was seventy years ago; the battle for Troy, some thirty centuries earlier. Those times are not mine, and experiences in a hospital are only metaphorically like those of battle. Still, I've been bolstered by both my father and the poet in my confrontation with leukemia.

Across the intervening centuries, Homer seems quite contemporary in his charting of the interplay between the social and the existential that colors our inevitable meeting with death. Despite being god-like descendants of earlier, greater races of men, his heroes are highly attuned to the vulnerabilities of life, exquisitely aware of their fragile mortality. Death, that incurable bitterness, casts its shadow on them, even in their moments of glory, and while heroism may gain renown, it affords no salvation. Not even godlike Achilles, for all his might, will escape the darkness. We are all like Homer's heroes who, despite their prayers and sacrifices, cannot deflect fate. In the end, we can only control how we meet the lot the gods assign us. My father was such a hero, and I strive to be one as well.

If I lose my battle with leukemia, having contested it bravely, my renown will reside in the memories of my family first and then my friends. My life will in time be forgotten, but perhaps for a while, remembrance of it will be a comfort, a teaching, or a gift.

WHAT MY PARENTS
TAUGHT ME

Recently I received a letter from the past. It bore a return address I knew well, 103 Grant Avenue, Glens Falls, NY. During my reunion visit, I had stood before that house under the maple tree I'd helped my father plant when we first moved in. The family living there now had somehow found my seventh-grade report card. With some Internet sleuthing, they located me in Houston and sent it on. My mother's signatures acknowledged receipt of my grades for two marking periods—generally excellent, but a few slips in music and art, both vital parts of my life today. Another portal to the past, the yellowed, slightly tattered card took me back to my childhood days.

During my return to my hometown, I'd walked the streets of my childhood in a widening circuit that roughly correlated with my age. First I toured the few blocks around my grandmother's house. Across the street and five houses toward town lived a family whose daughter was my age. Nancy and I often played in the yard by the side of her house, which is now covered by an extension to the garage. But as if to confirm the strangeness of memory, I felt I was there in a different time. I was sitting on a fence topped with iron pipe looking up to the steps to her back door. Nancy's mother opens it and steps out onto the porch. "Children," she says, "President Roosevelt is dead." I remembered the scene, her tone of voice, her gray dress, the steps from the porch to the driveway with their white paint peeling, the pipe pressed against the backs of my thighs, even the direction I was facing, but nothing else about our play that day. Nothing before and nothing after. Yet these few moments were so clear and present.

At that moment I again thought about being with Nancy, the stream of memory began its fitful flow, casting up one remembrance after another. I found myself tracing paths to other friends, to the games played, to lying on our backs eating wild rhubarb, to licking iron pipes when the winter gripped the town, to jumping out windows into the snow to shovel drifts away from the front door, to once putting a firecracker in the mouth of a frog . . . all memories encompassed in the collage that represents my past.

On the way to the reunion hotel for dinner, I passed by the elementary school where I entered kindergarten at age five. When I first went to school, my mother walked some seven blocks along Sherman Avenue to the major street crossing, where a volunteer parent ushered us across and onto the school grounds. After several test runs, my mother turned me loose. I set off on my epic journey and returned in triumph. I later learned that a neighborly party line was keeping me under surveillance, one neighbor after another reporting to my mother a spotting of me on the way past. But walking to and from school, I felt very brave.

As I continued my reunion walk, I passed the duplex in which we'd lived when my father returned from the war. It has been remade as a florist/gift shop. There my parents had assigned me two tasks: to pour off the cream from the bottled milk delivered to our porch and to knead the red pellet into the oleo to give it the semblance of butter. I also took piano lessons from a woman who lived below us.

I made my way to our house on Grant Avenue, recalling how my childhood world expanded. When school didn't dictate my schedule, I'd often go out with only a vague notion of what lay ahead. During the summer, I might be playing basketball or baseball, or in winter, skating on a large pond in some woods that bordered the town. Or anytime, I might just be hanging out with friends. In high school, after supper, boys and girls together usually rode our bikes to one of several gathering places. We felt unencumbered and unobserved. But looking back, I know the neighborhood remained watchful. As a computer scientist, I envision a wide-area social network tracking me and my friends, giving us broad compass for our activities, but guarding against possible overreaching. During my high-school years, that guard proved imperfect. Freedom exacted a price: the car crash that killed a classmate, the prom queen who got pregnant, and alcohol abuse that disrupted several young lives.

My report card called to mind another school, the Montessori School my daughters attended. One night, I sat scrunched in a child's chair in a classroom, while one of their teachers proudly held forth on the freedom given her charges in the school. None of the ordinary restrictions of rows of desks, she said, and no lessons in lockstep. Children explored materials and lessons freely, with only the lightest touch of their teachers to guide them. Like my teenage gatherings, perhaps.

When the meeting was over, however, we went out into a gated parking lot watched over by a guard. Inside, the kids may have been free to explore, but the fences and the guard signified that on the periphery, dangers loomed. More guarding, protecting, anticipating the unpleasant. To what degree should we grant our children freedom in a world so seemingly fraught with danger?

Of course, Houston bears little relationship to my small hometown of seventy years ago. Parents have good reasons nowadays to be on alert regarding their children's comings and goings. But my mother and father would have been bemused by today's "helicopter parents," who hover over their children's activities, even into the college years. Within what boundaries should our children learn what they need to know?

Like many parents of their generation, mine promoted hard work, civic responsibility, honesty, and other widely accepted virtues. Their teachings, however, were implicit. They seldom spoke directly about these important matters. Instead, their lives were their teachings. In time, I learned what they wanted to convey.

But it took some time. My parents freely commented on many less consequential aspects of my life. Perhaps they had read Ralph Waldo Emerson, who said consistency is the hobgoblin of little minds. In any event, they allowed their opinions wide latitude. They were clearly proud of me. They praised my academic and athletic achievements. But when I got a 95 on a test, my father would ask, "Who got 100?" In high school, when I started out the door on a Friday night, my mother might say, "You need to change your clothes." When I countered that all my friends would be similarly dressed, her response would be, "We don't care what others do." Yet, in another situation, my father might flip this argument, "You don't see Eddy doing that, do you?" To me, their praise and advice seemed contingent and tempered by doubt.

My parents, however, upheld a mixture of duty and stoicism that never wavered. This, more than any other, was their teaching. It is one I learned well. As a child, I often heard them say, "No one wants to hear your troubles." In later years, I attributed this belief to life during the Great Depression and the Second World War. Then everyone had something to complain about. No one wanted to be additionally burdened with another's complaints. Had we a family crest, this would likely have been our motto.

A few times I asked my father about his limp. His answer was always the same. "Oh, it's nothing." But, of course, it was not nothing. It was German shrapnel that hadn't been or couldn't be removed. A simple statement that explains the matter. But one, I guess, that could be taken a preamble to a plea for sympathy. And he never would make such a plea.

My mother developed breast cancer when I was about thirteen. She went to the hospital "for a few days." My father told me that she was sick. And in a few days, she came home. Then back for several more visits. Finally, she returned, cured. I knew nothing of the radical mastectomy that took not only her breast, but lymph nodes as well. An operation that scarred her deeply.

I first sensed the extent at a dinner with family friends. Their two children and I were settled in at the end of a long table, my parents and their hosts at the other. My father was standing, commanding attention as he often did. He grabbed half a loaf of bread and held it to his chest. It stuck out like a single breast. I didn't hear what he said, but I do recall laughter. A shudder, however, went through me, as a shadow of what had happened to my mother passed over me.

In the years that followed, whenever she spoke of the operation, she made it seem like a brief inconvenience. She never mentioned pain or suffering. But when she swam, I could see the glint of the safety pin that held a padded cup somewhat loosely in her suit. In those days, I guess, that passed for reconstruction. The cup didn't conceal the scars that ran to her armpit. Its obvious presence seemed another aspect of her disregard for her looks. Don't dwell on your suffering.

When I was in graduate school in California, my habit was to call my parents each Sunday. Our conversations were rather formulaic, but they did connect us across the country. If my father answered, he would quickly turn the phone over to my mother. She was the one to gather information. But she shared some of it only grudgingly. On one occasion, when I asked how things were going in Florida, she said all was fine as usual, now that they had settled down.

A clue that something was going on. "Settled down from what?" I asked.

"Oh, nothing. Well, not much. Your father was in the hospital for a couple of days, but he's fine now."

"In the hospital? For what?" I worried.

"Well, he had a small operation. A simple one." she assured me. "He's fine and back home. Out by the pool now."

It was like pulling teeth. "Operation for what?" I pressed.

"He had colon cancer," she finally relented. "But it's fine now, as I say. They removed it. Got it all."

And so it had gone. Never burden someone else with your problems. As I said, our family motto. If we could have a two-part motto, we would add: Never let your problems keep you from doing your duty.

That I am my parents' child was made strikingly clear to me some years ago during a soccer game between two high-powered teenage teams. My daughter leapt to head a ball. An opponent tried the same, but instead of the ball, she hit Meghan's face with the back of her head. With a cry, my daughter went face down on the pitch. Along with her trainer, I ran to her.

As she turned over, I urged her on. "Get up, Meghan. Get back in the game. You can do it. Your team needs you."

The trainer looked at me in alarm. "What are you talking about? Her nose is probably broken. I'm taking her out!"

As Meghan was led off—yes, with a broken nose—my wife turned away from me as though I had done something shameful. And, of course, I had. But my reaction had come unbidden. My parents had prepared me for moments like this. Had I been on the ground with a broken nose, they would have urged me to play on under the banner of stoicism and duty.

Fortunately, other memories are short, and it is only in mine that the soccer incident lingers. Neither my daughter, whose nose healed uneventfully, nor my wife seems to remember much about it. But I remember it well, and I know what it means.

A few years later, at a track stadium, I saw my daughter Kate pay a steep price to honor a commitment to her college team. She was an outstanding runner, winner of a number of conference championships. This year, she was recovering from an injury and hadn't been competing. If she skipped this last meet, she would retain a full year of eligibility. But the competition in the meet would be intense, and Rice needed all the points it could get.

As the preparations for the 10,000 meters began, I could see her jogging beside the track. Then she took her place at the starting line. She won the race. As she finished, I felt happy for her accomplishment. I also recognized its cost. A year of eligibility lost in one race. A price she paid for her team. I was proud of her.

Much of my conduct when I was young was, of course, shaped by what my parents told me. But as I aged, I felt less constrained by their admonitions. In my interests and career, I moved quite far from the path they envisioned for me. From time to time, I thought my vantage point gave me a better view of life than theirs. But looking back, I wonder.

Have I taught my daughters to bear their burdens and do their duty? I don't lecture them on duty and responsibility. But in repeated returns to the past, I have seen how many teachings are unspoken. In important matters, it is often deed rather than word that teaches. In the way they faced death, my parents became my teachers of life again. Now that I live in death's shadow, the way I confront my fate will be a teaching for my girls. It should be a lesson about living.

CHINGACHGOOK

On the second day of my reunion, I drove again to the lake. Passing the Knob, I kept on the roadway that followed the shore. A few miles on, I reached Camp Chingachgook. When I was eight, my parents sent me there for two weeks. The warriors, the campfire, and the ceremony made my first night as a camper exhilarating.

Led by an Iroquois brave as night fell, we campers trekked in a silent single file though the woods. Trees arching overhead darkened our way, but ahead we saw his flickering torch. Occasionally, the path crossed a clearing under brightening stars. We emerged from the forest at the edge of the lake, where our leader settled us in a circle around a fire pit. Another warrior with feathered headdress stepped from the trees and into the clearing. He chanted a hymn to the Great Spirit, and soon, from out on the lake, a war canoe with several Indians slid quietly toward us over the still water. When it reached the shore, one Indian stood, drew back his bow, and launched an arrow high over our heads. With a roar, from the trees above and behind us, fire flashed down. The fire pit exploded in flame. The braves, now with shields and spears, leapt from the canoe and ran several times around our circle before disappearing into the forest. When their war cries faded, the warrior with the headdress, turning slowly around to look hard at each of us, began a story of hunters and wolves. When he looked at me, I was transported to another world.

I returned to Camp Chingachgook after so many years to find the entrance framed by an impressive arch of wood and stone from which hung a sign with the camp's name emblazoned in gold letters. A far cry from what I remembered from my camping days, when a board lettered in paint and nailed to a pole pointed the way in. The modest structure that had once served as camp headquarters had been replaced by a building that looked like a resort lodge with a grand porch and ground-level patio.

The Welcome Center was on the second floor of the main building. However, on this autumn afternoon, no welcome awaited me. The camp was closed. Behind a large glass pane, an array of photographs showed busy campers in a variety of summer activities. Canoeing was still featured, but no headdresses, feathered shields, wampum beads figured in today's pictures.

The camp of long ago was divided into two sections separated by a dining hall and craft center. In the Lower Camp, for campers under twelve, were six tents, each named for an Iroquois tribe. Along with five other boys, I was assigned to the Oneida tent with Dan, a college student, as our counselor. Carlos from Cuba, one of my tentmates, was the youngest of all the campers. I was the second youngest. The others in my tent were eleven and twelve. Three of them had come to camp as friends.

Early days were engaging and exciting. The spectacular welcoming ceremony, which I recalled so vividly, then the next day: swimming, a version of Capture the Flag, and beginning craft projects. Good food with storytelling after dinner. A great beginning. The days that followed, however, proved less wonderful.

I became the butt of various jokes fomented by Poochie, Larry, and Shorty, my three tentmates from the same school in Schenectady. Simple stuff at first: a frog in my bed, my shoelaces tied in knots, my swim towel covered with mud. Why me? Why not Carlos? I didn't know.

I considered seeking help from Dan, but he seemed friendlier to the three than to Carlos and me. Perhaps we were just too young for him. Then, too, while their smirks announced them as the instigators, there was no evidence to convict them. Finally, I already knew that our family bore our trials without complaint. These considerations kept me silent.

I hoped that I was passing through an initiation, after which Poochie, Larry, and Shorty would welcome me as a friend. For a week or so, that hope seemed justified. While the three were not overtly friendly, they stopped their harassment. Still, I was constantly on the watch for pranks. The unmitigated fun of the first days was now shadowed by continual wariness.

At the end of the first week, my parents arrived for an afternoon visit. "How are you doing?" they wanted to know. Of course, I knew their hopes that I was having a wonderful time. So in keeping with our family way, I made no complaint. They left, certain that camp was a great experience for me. I saw them drive away, reminding myself that I had only one more week to go.

For some time, I had been working on my crafts project—a decorated Indian shield. Quite an undertaking: Bending a sapling under water for several days to make a circular frame. Cutting the covering canvas and painting it with Indian symbols. Securing the cover to the frame with leather lashes. In the end, it was a grand construction. I was very proud of my work, finished a day before camp ended.

When my parents had taken my gear to the car, I announced my surprise. Wait, I said, and ran to the crafts house. There was my shield. Not on the peg on which it had hung, but on the floor, its frame broken and its canvas slashed and daubed with black paint. I don't remember how I hid my loss from my parents. I believe they mistook my moroseness for sadness that I was leaving camp. I do recall one image from our departure: Shorty and Poochie standing at the edge of the parking lot laughing, each with his hands making a large oval then squeezing them into fists as though crushing a shield.

I never told my parents about my difficulties at camp. Instead I always supported their view that it had been a very good experience for me. Unfortunately that meant that they were eager to send me back the next summer. Off I went, hoping that practical jokes and meanness would target someone else. As I watched the campers roll in, I was tense. But none of my three bullies appeared. I enjoyed two weeks at Chingachgook.

For several years, I bore a scar from the harassment of the first year. You wouldn't see it, but I felt it every time I saw the camp picture that I kept in a shoebox in my closet. There we are, campers and counselor seated in from of the Oneida tent. We're all smiling. For some time, the photo made me ashamed, because despite our age differences, I am almost as big as my tormentors. Carlos is small, but I am not. Why didn't I stand up for myself? Why did I let them push me around? The easy excuse—that they were three years older—didn't sit well, particularly when viewed from a teenage vantage point. But in time, my feelings settled, and the memory of Chingachgook faded.

Until one afternoon in late summer before I went off to college. My friend Ellen and I were sitting on her dock on Lake George, waiting for others to bring a boat for waterskiing. On the next dock, some forty feet way, another couple were putting some supplies into a canoe. The guy waved to us, and Ellen called, "Hey, Shorty!" I looked closely. Could it be? Believing is seeing.

"Shorty Robinson?" I asked her.

"Right," she replied. "Do you know him?"

"Renewing acquaintances," I mumbled and walked back up the dock.

I followed the path along the shore to the other dock and turned out onto it.

"Are you Shorty?" I asked when I reached him.

"Right. Shorty Robinson, Bobby. Who are you?" he said.

Looking down at him, I could see why he'd retained his nickname.

"Chingachgook," I said and jammed my forearm into his chest. He stumbled back and fell off the end of the dock into the lake. The girl with him screamed and ran from the dock. I could hear Ellen yelling something from across the way.

He stood in the shallow water, sputtering and shaking his head. "What the hell is this? Who are you?" he demanded. He started to scramble out, but looking at me, he had second thoughts. Time had changed our relation. I was now the bigger, stronger one.

I leaned over the end of the dock and offered him a hand. "It's about a shield and long ago. Come on back up. No more trouble," I said.

By now Ellen had reached the dock to grab me and provide a character reference for Shorty.

"What's the matter with you? Are you crazy? He's my friend, a really good guy. What the hell are you doing?"

While Ellen firmly held me, Shorty warily climbed out.

I told my story as he dried off. He remembered his part in it.

Sheepishly, he admitted to harassment, but he pleaded a kind of statute of limitations. He charged me with an unprovoked attack. I admitted to carrying a grudge too long. We settled our score with the understanding that we both had done things that we wished we could undo.

Our waterski boat arrived, and Shorty and I parted. I never saw him again. I must confess, however, I still feel a bit of satisfaction in reliving our last encounter. There he goes again, backwards off the dock into the water.

BIRDS AND BEES

Love is the answer, but while you are waiting for
the answer, sex raises some pretty good questions.
—*Woody Allen*

Of course, there were many things my parents didn't
or couldn't or wouldn't teach me. The morning
after the reunion dinner, in front of an old church, I
thought of one dramatic lesson they left to others. I'd
been away from that Presbyterian church for fifty years,
but its streaked gray exterior had resisted the corrosion
of time. The church apparently had aged enough and
now refused to get any older. Even the door to the fellowship room seemed unaltered from my sixth-grade
days, when many of my classmates and I had gathered

for monthly meetings. Our group was led by a young married couple who offered us games, food, and counsel on the teenage life that loomed before us.

Now, shaking my head and laughing, I attracted the attention of a man raking the lawn nearby.

"Can I help you?" he called to me.

"No, thanks. I'm back for a high school reunion. Just remembering when I used to go here," I chuckled.

"Are you still a Presbyterian? I mean, somewhere else."

"No, and I wasn't then. There used to be a meeting for kids in sixth grade. It didn't matter what your religion was. Well, let me take that back. My father was Catholic and my mother Presbyterian. So you were half right. I'm not much of anything now."

"Well," said the raker, "you're still welcome. Enjoy yourself."

"Thanks," I replied. "I'm having a good time. I've been away a long time, but I remember some great days here."

In truth, however, I had one particular day in mind. A day of chaos for the kids and disaster for the fellowship leaders. As I headed back to my hotel, I recalled the path we sixth-grade boys had taken to a bizarre final meeting of the youth fellowship. And how we'd dealt with the aftermath. It all seemed like a crazy, but oddly apt metaphor for life.

One autumn afternoon, I bounded up the short flight of stairs to my room. Throwing my books aside, I dove onto my bed and called to my dog Champ, who was trailing not far behind. With a pull from me and the digging of his back paws in the bedspread, the dog clambered onto the bed. For a short time, we rolled around. I hid my face from Champ's sloppy kisses. When he finally settled down, I pulled a comic book from the bedside stand. Champ stretched out watching me with his tail still twitching. For a while, I read while he rested in anticipation.

After ten minutes, I abruptly sat up. Grabbing my baseball glove and ruffling the dog's head, I announced it was time for a walk. He leapt from the bed and started twisting about eagerly.

Pushing him from in front of my small bookcase, I reached to put my comic away. There was a book I'd never before seen. A slim, brown volume entitled *Birds and Bees*. I was at first confused, because on the book's cover was a photograph of a dog, looking somewhat like Champ, sitting up with raised paws as though begging for food.

What's up with this? I wondered. Probably some nature book. More educational encouragement from Mom and Dad. Probably Mom, who'd like the perky dog. With no more thought, I tossed the book onto its shelf and bolted out of my room and down the stairs with Champ barking happily at my heels. Through the back door, across the grass we ran.

A well-worn path brought us to the baseball diamond. Hardly a diamond. Just smoother ground that had been picked quite clean of rocks and divots by successive generations of young ball players. Behind home plate, which was marked by chalk, a chain link fence kept wild pitches and most foul balls out of a shallow ravine that edged one side of the field. Other than this constraint, the field opened in all directions. By convention, a sawhorse and several old chairs marked the outfield boundary. The bases, too, were marked with chalk, which needed frequent replenishment in the summer, when games went many innings.

We arrived just in time for the elaborate ritual of choosing teams. Lots of baseball, and lots of talking, not just at choosing up, but between innings and after the game. But on this day, the conversation kept returning to something very odd that had happened at school. A puzzle had been posed for which we had no sure answer.

Recess had begun as usual, with boys and girls bursting out of school doors to romp on the playground. Linda had playfully punched John in the shoulder, which set off a cascade of chasing, tagging, pushing, and screaming. All the kids were in high gear, until Miss Morse, the large, fearsome gym teacher, suddenly blew her whistle. She wore it on a leather lanyard, the one she used to whip our legs when we misbehaved. Several times she blew shrilly, bringing the playground chaos to a halt.

"All sixth-grade girls, come with me!" she commanded.

Those girls looked at each other, puzzled, but Miss Morse meant business. Again, she ordered them into the gym. So they shuffled together into a ragged line and followed her docilely through the door. They remained there until recess was almost over.

On their return, there was none of their usual laughter or gossiping. Instead, looking somewhat stunned, they wandered off in small, tight groups. Gail, who boys grudgingly acknowledged was the fastest runner in the class, turned down a challenge. She was heard telling one of them she wouldn't be racing again.

What had happened to the girls? None of us knew for sure, although a number proposed theories. The idea of alien invasion, although exciting, was quickly discarded. Better ideas seemed to come from boys with older sisters. They announced that the meeting involved "a coming change," but they could offer few details. One boy asserted that the girls would be getting something called a "period." His sister had hers, but again, he knew nothing else.

The next day during recess, the conversation from the diamond continued. A few of us gathered under the large elm tree at the back of the playground. For a short time, we were out of Miss Morse's range. Apart from the usual turmoil, the sixth-grade girls stood quietly in small clusters as though they had nothing at all to do. Their stillness added urgency to our questioning.

What had we learned since yesterday? A number of clues had been found. First, a period involved blood in some way. One of the guys remembered his sister crying and running from the room with a stain on her skirt. Another boy was sure that girls put pads or napkins on to hold back the bleeding. He'd seen one his older sister had discarded in the trash. But, he said, the bleeding did stop after a while. He knew this from overhearing his sister tell a friend she was "off the rag." He gathered that this off-and-on sort of alternated. So, we concluded, once girls got on and off the rag, they must be more delicate. They shouldn't play hard; you couldn't knock them around.

Miss Morse was now headed our way, whistle raised to her lips. One of the boys offered a new, striking finding: the girls can stick some cotton thing in "down there" to keep the blood back. And then with a string, pull it out later. He'd seen one of these in the trash. To each of his listeners came the same question. "Stick it where?" But her whistle again blew sharply, and we scattered.

Soon, we were wrestling with shifty questions about babies—and how women produce them. Clearly, mothers carried babies inside, like Jack's mother who was expecting. The way she stuck out showed the baby had lots of room. Somehow by the time they became mothers, something momentous had to happen for a baby to get out. But what? And how? Mysteries within mysteries.

How were babies made? Obviously mothers and fathers cooperated in some way. Once I'd seen Champ mounting a female dog said to be in heat. And when Champ had been pulled off her, a feat requiring some kicking, I'd seen the change in Champ's equipment. What the boys would later call "the red rocket" had emerged from its furry case. One of the boys said he'd seen a bull doing the same to a cow, but the bull's rocket was "huge!" Could something like this happen with people? My imagination couldn't encompass my father on my mother's backside, thrusting at her like Champ on that girl dog. Or a bull on a cow!

Questions like these prompted me to retrieve the book with the begging dog on the cover. Perhaps its odd appearance on my shelf was in coordination with the girls' meeting in the gym. Talk for girls, books for boys. But the first few pages about the "wonders of life" offered no help. So I tossed the book aside, and tuned in "The Lone Ranger" on my crystal set.

The next day, more information, this time from one of the guys who claimed special knowledge. His father was a doctor many of the boys had seen carrying his bag to house calls around town. Although the doctor was always friendly, I was wary of him. Still vivid were memories of the shots I'd been given at my house when I was younger. As soon as I had seen the needle, I dove behind a large chair in the living room. It took my mother and uncle to disentangle me from its legs, drag me into view, and hold me steady while the doctor jabbed me—after pulling my pants down! Sore and humiliated, I had sulked in my room for the remainder of the afternoon, the offer of cookies notwithstanding.

But news from the doctor's son had to be taken seriously. He reported that his father had a machine for making babies. A woman wanting a child came to his father's office with some white stuff, kind of like the cream that floated at the top of milk bottles. She lay on a sofa. His father put his machine, a pump of some kind, down there. That's how the creamy stuff got in her. That's how she got a baby—my early and inadequate understanding of artificial insemination.

From the quick questions that spilled out, it was clear that there was much more to learn about this strange machine. So we charged the doctor's son with a kind of spying mission: to somehow see the machine in operation, to watch his father make a baby.

He promised to report back as soon as possible.

When we heard nothing further from him, our belief

in the machine faded. Some of the older guys asserted that no machine at all was involved. All a guy had to do was "thump 'em" or "screw 'em" to get the job done. Still, our interest in female anatomy persisted, and our puzzlement regarding it remained great. It was this combination that prompted what I later thought of as the "Tampax caper."

During recess, one of my friends called a meeting of the investigative team. Under the trees at the back of the playground, he produced a scrap of paper, which he'd recovered in one of his frequent examinations of his older sister's trash. From what could be read, the boys quickly saw that it was part of a package insert for Tampax. It included part of a diagram, incomplete, but suggesting a diagram or map of the mysterious terrain. What we needed, we decided, was the complete picture. Then we could see if girls had three holes or two, a question prompting lots of argument. Maybe we could discover how the white stuff got in. How babies avoided the piss. And even how girls got thumped or screwed.

The conservative approach was to scout for another Tampax box, one with a complete package insert. But eager and anxious, we soon devised a quicker plan. Bobby and I were dispatched to the local drug store to steal a Tampax box.

Bobby engaged the counter girl with a special order of a coffee ginger ale. He hoped the choice would distract her, while I started toward the magazine rack. Ducking behind it, I looked for the section I'd once heard his mother call "feminine products." After a couple false starts, I began to worry. So I joined Bobby at the counter and ordered my own drink, a coke float.

Then, mumbling about forgetting something, I scurried down a different aisle, almost running into the Tampax display. Gingerly lifting a box from the shelf, I stuffed into my pants under my shirt.

As I stood up, however, I felt a large hand on my shoulder. The druggist!

"What are you doing? This isn't the place for you," he said.

"Oh, nothing," I said, shaking a bit. "Bobby, uh, rolled my quarter on the floor, and I thought it came over this way. But I guess not."

"Well, I don't see any quarters around here. On your way now."

"Right, sir," I chirped and headed back to the counter.

We finished our drinks at the counter and with muffled laughter scampered out the door with the precious map in the box tucked safely under my shirt.

The next day, Saturday, the boys gathered at the baseball diamond. Choosing up took second place to the examination of the map, which, now whole, offered its own picture of the place in question. Although still a drawing, it quickly resolved the question of three holes or two. But the space, outlined like a small lake, certainly couldn't contain a baby. It could, however, as the instructions clearly indicated, accommodate the Tampax itself, once it had entered the lake from one side and been released with the plunger somehow.

Soon the boys made a connection with their own stiffenings. Thumping, screwing, and the rest must mean putting their equipment in there in some way, like inserting a Tampax. Our investigations were getting us closer, but we had a way to go.

It was then that Don and Sue Middlebach, leaders of a youth group at the First Presbyterian Church, appeared. In their desire to recruit young boys and girls, Don and Sue had trimmed religious overtones from their program. Even Catholics and Jews joined the monthly meetings at the church. Good food, games, and easy conversation enticed us. The Middlebachs were welcoming and approachable. They asked us to call them by their first names, in sharp contrast to the usual adult admonition to be polite. Finally, they gave boys and girls an excuse to mingle again.

At a meeting that would be the last, while we plowed through our dinners, Don set up a 16mm projector. Sue opened a screen at the front of the room. After dessert, as Don threaded the projector, he announced that we were going to see a movie about one of the most important aspects of life. Sue herded us into chairs, where we sorted ourselves, boys on the left, girls on the right of a dividing aisle. She dimmed the lights. The projector began its clicking. It splashed a flickering countdown from ten to one.

The title spread across a field of waving flowers: "The Miracle of Life." It lingered for a while, then dissolved to a homey scene, where two young children sat between their parents on the sofa in a pleasantly furnished room. I fidgeted. Not a film version of that book at home, I hoped. I was encouraged when I heard the end of a question: "... where do babies come from?" Count on Don and Sue to resolve uncertainty, to bring resolution to the debates and speculation that had so consumed us during the past month. More at ease, I settled deeply into my chair, intent on the screen.

The scene changed. Now a man and a woman stood facing each other from opposite sides of the picture. No children. Smiling, the couple moved together and embraced. He gently kissed her. While a repressed chorus of grunts and moans stirred on our side, little noise came from the girls.

The scene again changed. Now the couple had stepped back from one another, and each had been replaced by a drawing. The camera zoomed in on the woman, focusing on the area below her waist. Her clothes dropped away, revealing a hairless diagram much like a lake with two channels entering at one end. But this map was animated. While the narrator talked of sperm, a number of them were shown, apparently swimming in the lake, headed for a destination on the side opposite the entry. The boys began to squirm, but some of the girls, as though possessing superior knowledge, nodded wisely to one another.

I was so taken by the animated map that I lost track of the narrator's voice. Suddenly, the focus switched to the man, zooming in on him as it had on the woman. Hairless, in plain view, his flaccid penis hung over his testicles. Now the girls squirmed, and some buried their heads in their arms. But there was more. The picture morphed into one in which the formerly limp penis was now stiffly erect, even more than erect, slightly tilted upward. It spanned the screen.

Girls cried out in horror. Boys guffawed. A few girls headed for the exits. We boys started pushing and punching and shouting. By the time Don was able to shut the projector down, the now giant penis had entered the lake, pressing the shore all around. Sue stood in front, trying to block the image while she explained a mix-up in films, but few kids remained to hear her.

We rushed to the courtyard in front of the church, where we again established our segregation—boys on one side of a tile walk, girls on the other. Each group watched the other warily. Then, as if on signal, our two assemblies melted away along the side streets that bounded the church property.

Out into the future we spilled. In a few years, we boys would be like treasure hunters, uncertain of what we were seeking and how it might be reached. Whispers and gossip guided us, at times on quite different paths. In the dark, we might lay hands on part of the treasure, but for a long time, like blind men, we were unsure how to make sense of what we'd touched. The exciting and strange tactile knowledge we gained added little to our understanding of what really lay beneath.

Further explorations on sofas, behind garages, and in the woods added bits to my understanding. But breakthroughs were few. Slow learning by doing persisted, although rumors suggested that certain girls would willingly accelerate the process. By now, however, my desire to "have sex" was mixed with fear that I might actually confront the opportunity. No heroics for me.

During this time, other than sliding a book unremarked into my bookcase, my parents added nothing to my woeful stock of knowledge about these matters. I was reluctant, indeed unable to ask for help. After all, my mother was a girl. And I was still wary of my father, the War Hero.

THE CHAMP

Although other houses had been built in the neighborhood of my childhood home during my long absence, some of the paths to the small mountains were still open. These paths had been avenues to adventure for two dogs, my Champ and a neighbor's dog, Boots, the love of his life. Each morning throughout the early 1950s, the dogs sat on their respective back porches staring intently at one another across two yards split by an unkempt stretch that divided our property from our backyard neighbors where Boots lived. I see Champ's tail quivering, not quite wagging in anticipation. Boots is too distant for me to see any tail-twitching on her part. But from having watched this ritual many times, I know she was revving up. Then, they suddenly burst whatever bonds that hold them. They bolt from their porches, each with a joyful bark and dash toward one another. When they hit the scruffy divide, they abruptly stop, as always, nose to nose. Usually they next begin a wild dance, darting toward and away from each other or tossing and tugging on a stick. In winter, their dance consists of rolling in the snow and jumping on one another.

In late summer and autumn, after a minute of still-ness, a burst of energy propels them west along the dividing track toward the low mountains a mile away. It is as though in their brief quiet, they had planned the day's doings. Once underway, they are unlikely to return before dusk.

In the early 1950s, near the edge of our modest town, few fences constrained canine exuberance. And this pair had discovered ways around the fences that might have hemmed them in. On autumn afternoons, Champ and I often arrived home at about the same time: I, from football practice, and the dog, from who knows what. He sometimes brought evidence of his recent activities. Among these were rolling in mud and running through plants that enlisted him in spreading their seeds, or worse, their burrs. Occasionally ticks returned with him, or a leech or two. Because he and Boots were both short-haired, ridding them of these unwelcome attachments wasn't too difficult. Hosing, a scrub brush, and perhaps some tweezers were usually sufficient. My father liked to burn the leeches with his cigarette. Both dogs acqui-esced to treatment, even the burning, as though it was a reasonable payment for a day of rollicking in the hills.

Encounters with porcupines were a different matter. When one of the dogs returned with a snout embedded with quills, extraction was required. The dogs seemed to realize that pawing wouldn't get the job done, but they still shrank from the pliers my father brandished. Moaning and groaning proved of little avail. He approached the afflicted dog with urgency. The job had to be done, and it had to be done now. The dog shook, but submitted.

Neither Boots nor Champ was a quick study where porcupines were involved. But fortunately such encounters were rare, and we saw their unpleasant consequences only a few times each year. Because of my father's travels, quill removal occasionally fell to my mother. She attacked the problem in much the way my father did: no nonsense. And the dogs deferred to her in roughly the way they had to my father. When I was twelve, or so, my father made me his alternate for quill removal. The dogs recognized that I lacked his gravitas and even the gravitas of my mother. Their twisting and howling made it clear that if they had to suffer, they wanted to suffer at a parent's hand. But my father wanted me to do the job. So at his command, I clamped a quill, worked it around to snip off the barb, and then pulled it out or pushed it through the snout. The dogs and I suffered, but I learned my job, and they granted me a kind of canine certification.

I received my award after the third or fourth quill removal session. Before, when I'd finished, Champ would skulk off with only the briefest look back at me. This time, however, running up the stairs, I called back to him. In a minute, Champ trailed slowly, not far behind. Ruffling his head, I announced, "Time to take a walk, fella!" Now I was speaking Champ's language. Down the stairs with Champ barking happily at my heels. Out the back door we went. All was forgiven.

Porcupines were not the worst of the dangers of the fields and hills. The tracks the dogs ran crossed several streets before leaving the edge of town. When cars and dogs sped across the same space, metal trumped flesh. One afternoon, Boots came limping back at dusk with Champ solicitous at her side. A raw red patch on her right rear leg recorded her glancing encounter with some vehicle. Her owners cleaned her wound and rigged a bandage that she barely tolerated. For a few days, with Champ at her side, she lay in the soft autumn sun. Soon she was stretching, and not much later was running again.

Champ had his own encounter with danger. One day he returned limping. My father concluded that he had been grazed not by a car, but by a bullet. Somebody had shot and barely wounded him. In his recovery, he followed Boots: a few days of lounging in the sun and then back to the hills. Now, however, when I saw the two head out, I felt a twinge of alarm. A shadow had fallen on what had before would have seemed a great frolic. But the dogs took no more heed of looming dangers than they had of porcupine quills. Off they went.

One afternoon, when I returned from school, Champ was pacing in our kitchen. From time to time, he stopped to paw at the back door. My mother told me that Boots had been killed, hit by a car on one of the roads that ran along the fields on the edge of town. A neighbor had found Champ standing by her body and called her owner. He had retrieved her body and Champ.

The next morning I stepped out onto our back porch.

Champ started to eager attention and followed me. Time passed without Boots' appearance. Champ began pacing back and forth. I went into the yard and called to him. He came toward me, wagging his tail. Then he stopped. He peered at me as though he thought I might have her hidden behind my back. When he realized she was not with me, he turned and trotted back to our porch, where he sat expectantly for the rest of the morning.

For a few weeks, he followed a routine—sitting, pacing, sitting again, then leaving the porch and disappearing for much of the day. One day, before he left the porch, he barked at me several times. He howled once. It was too much. I stopped letting him onto the back porch.

In time, he abandoned his vigil. But he was a changed dog. Outside, he stayed close to our house, where I'd see him lying under bushes or the maple tree in our front yard. Inside, he followed one of us from room to room. In a year, he became an old dog.

With the coming of spring, about six months after Boots' death, I walked with Champ through the fields toward the mountains, although he seemed to have lost interest in such outings. Our walks became shorter and shorter as he more quickly turned back to home. I settled for a slow lap around our yard, but that soon became too much.

And then that day of sadness. Standing there, years later, before our house, I could see the garage in which Champ spent his last day, lying on soft pile of blankets, unable to move much but his head.

We hovered around him in slow acceptance of the inevitable. Finally, my parents agreed it was time to put him down. I expected that meant my father would take him to the vet for the procedure. But no, I was to go with him. On that hot August day, I was there when Champ was put to sleep.

With my father at my side, I carried Champ from our car to the animal hospital. In my arms, his eyes were veiled. They'd barely flickered when, with steps careful and slow like his, I mounted the hospital's sun-blasted porch, where flowers drooped in neglected pots and a window unit throbbed. I stood at the door, uncertain and fearful, with his matted fur pressed hot against my chest. With his arm on my back my father moved me on. The cicadas shrilled an alien song as he opened the door and we stepped inside.

Champ lay on the table as though in sleep. Several times he shuddered—chasing rabbits in a dream with Boots perhaps. But I could see it was a plastic tube piercing his leg that cruelly unsettled his rest. I shuddered, too, feeling his life take slow downward steps: no breath, no dream, no pulse, no dog.

After, I stroked those furry bones as though they might move again. But they lay impossibly still, while a deepening chill pervaded the room. The cold suddenly seized me. I stumbled up and fled out to the porch, leaving my father and Champ behind. On the porch, shivering by the blistered pots, I waited for warmth to return.

The wailing of the cicadas rose in the sweltering air.

HELEN DYING

And all the winds go sighing,
For sweet things dying
—*Christina Rossetti*

When my father retired, my parents moved from Connecticut to Sarasota, Florida, where they lived with a pleasant view of a golf course. On a visit in early June 1991, however, I squinted in the reflected whiteness of the Sarasota Memorial Hospital as I pulled into one of its few open parking spaces. My mother was in there. She'd suffered from weakness and severe headaches for a week, or perhaps a month, before her physician had admitted her. He hadn't known of her condition until a few days ago, because she believed no one wants to hear about your problems. This claim apparently extended to doctors. I was surprised that my father had even let me know she was sick.

When I called, my father began with the usual evasions. But I ferreted out the truth—that my mother was very ill. For almost forty years, remnants of breast cancer may have resided within her. Maybe that was the cause of her hospitalization. In any event, I'd flown to Sarasota as soon as possible. After dropping my bag at their house and squeezing what information I could from my father, who seemed overwhelmed, I drove to the hospital.

With directions from the receptionist, I found my mother's room. She lay looking out a small window at the slanting light. She hadn't heard me enter. I stood still, watching her. The sheet draped over her and the IV drip in her arm marked her as someone removed from everyday life. But something about the position of her body suggested she was unchanged. When she turned at my greeting, her dark brown eyes glowed with life, and her broad smile confirmed her vital presence.

"Oh, you shouldn't have come all this way," she began. Then dispensing with family protocol, she put out her hand for mine, and said, "I am so glad you're here."

"Mom, dear Mom," I softly said, taking her hand in mine.

Her deeply tanned and bruised arms stood out against the starched white of her bedding. Her wrinkles, etched, she claimed, from years of laughing, gave her an aged but ageless look. Had I not learned of her situation from my father, I'd have thought I'd interrupted a nap from which she would rise for a busy day. But cancer dwelled within. Perhaps old. Perhaps new. But metasta-sized in either case. An insidious marauder that would kill her.

Her hand was warm and dry. "How do you feel? I asked, trembling as I spoke.

"I'm all right," she replied. "I get some pain in my back, but they can give me medicine for that. I'm just tired." A few seconds passed. "But you know, I'm not going home. This is the last stop for me."

I wanted to protest, to tell her that there is always hope, to never give up. But I just stroked her hand. I knew what she knew. We were quiet for some time. Per-haps she dozed. Then a nurse came briskly in to check her vital signs. I found her perkiness offensive. How could she try to cheer up my mother given her cir-cumstances? Soon the nurse breezed out. "Have a nice night," she said as she exited.

My mother and I talked some more. She recounted her gradual slide into the hospital. First tiredness, then fatigue, then back and side pains, then headaches. A visit to the doctor and finally admission. A number of tests, the details of which she was uncertain about. The conclusion was unforgettable and unavoidable—termi-nal cancer. Very little time left.

"Look after your father," she said, gently squeezing my hand. "He needs me more than he knows. He should have died first. I would have been stronger without him than he'll be without me. Take care of him."

"I will," I replied. "I'll watch over him. I promise." I wasn't sure what I was agreeing to.

We passed a few minutes in silence. Then, as though speaking in her sleep, she said softly, "I've lived a wonderful life. You and your father . . . so good. I'm not afraid to die. You know, I never thought much about it. Oh, deaths in my family were very hard. My mother and father, brother and sisters. And when your father was fighting, I worried a lot about him—that he might get killed. But about myself, not much until the last month when I could tell I was in a bad way. Your father is terrified, but doesn't say much about it. But I'm different. I've always felt that whatever God there might be must be a God of love. When it's time, you just let go. Don't let them treat me any more. My life has been so good. I'll be OK."

I couldn't speak, even if I'd had something to say. The sun was setting, and she had almost fallen to sleep between sentences. Soon she slept. I waited for a few more minutes, and then decided she would be all right for the night. My father needed me as well. I left quietly.

ON NOT BEING CATHOLIC

As I reached the parking lot, the hospital lights came on, casting an eerie light on the surrounding trees. Her talk of a God of love set me to thinking about the odd place of religion in the life of my family. The argument, never overt, never ending.

When my parents met, my mother was Presbyterian and my father Catholic. During the war, when he was overseas, she occasionally took me to her church, a large assemblage of gray stone mottled by black stains and covered in places by layers of ivy. The main hall was the largest room I'd ever been in. Although the wooden pews were uncomfortable, and the service meant nothing to me, the airiness of the church, the lighted candles, and the echoes of the choir made the place another world. Because my mother made her church visits only on major holidays, I got to see the church at its most glorious.

But in the years following my father's return, she stopped taking me. She often said she was not a church-goer. In her view, God loved all people. The depth of his love was not influenced by where you sat on a particular day or what prayers you recited. For her, the path was clear, although sometimes difficult to follow. As Jesus said, be good to one another.

But with our few visits to the church, she had apparently anointed me a Presbyterian while my father was unable to object. If, when he returned, he had argued this choice, I never knew. On Sundays, while my parents stayed home, I sporadically attended Sunday school classes.

As I approached my teens, big questions arose to stir much wondering in me and my friends. Sex, of course, was at the top of our list. For some of my friends, religious matters found their way high on the list as well. Parents and teachers provided little, if any, instruction on sex. But churches were eager to explain the facts of religious life, although their explanations often seemed very different. These teachings got a few of us thinking about life and death, Heaven and Hell. And it got me and some others worrying.

When I was twelve, one of my best friends, Peter, was a Catholic. One day, he mentioned that he'd seen a picture of his baptism. He had cried when the priest sprinkled water on his head. I knew little of such an event. Peter explained that his baptism meant God would forgive his sins. This was a forgiveness that everyone needed. And Catholics had a way of getting it.

That night, I asked my mother if I had cried at my baptism. I was shocked to learn that I hadn't been baptized. Her disdain for such ceremonies did little to ease the deep fear that I felt. I had accumulated more than a decade of sins that wouldn't be wiped away. I might be headed to Hell. When I blurted that I wanted to be Catholic, my mother was unmoved.

"Catholicism," she said, "is a religion of fear. Who could believe in a God who created us so susceptible to sin and then punished us for falling short of perfection?"

"But Dad is Catholic," I protested. "Why shouldn't I be as well?"

"Your father is a wonderful man," she answered, "but you know he doesn't go to church. Do you think he'd be a better father if he spent an hour a week there? No. I admit he may believe some of that stuff. His mother is very religious. But you have to stand for yourself in a case like this."

Of course, had I stood for myself, I would have stood with Peter in the Catholic Church. I'd have signed up. But I resigned myself to the current arrangement. Neither of my parents would go to church. I would continue as a part-time Presbyterian. But my worries followed me through school and into my early college years. There, I began to speak of these matters as spiritual concerns.

During my sophomore year in college, I received a small package from my father, the first mail I could remember getting from him. A paperback book of the writings of Thomas Aquinas. No note, no comment. Just the book. Over the next few months, as I read parts of it, I puzzled over my father's intent. It wasn't a book he was likely to have read. I felt it was somewhat like a pamphlet conveyed by a door-to-door missionary. An invitation from Jehovah's Witnesses or another sect. But Thomas Aquinas? That seemed a bit much for an invitation to Catholicism.

When I was next at home, I asked him about the book.

"Now you're in college," he said, "it's good for you to learn about Catholicism. When you were a boy and we had more or less settled on part-time Presbyterianism for you, Catholicism never got a fair hearing." Then, almost as an afterthought, he said, "Your mother is now more open to it."

He ended our talk, saying that I should just give it some thought.

Before I returned to college, I told my mother about the book my father had sent me.

"Oh, she said, "he'll never give up on this. I wish he would, but he won't. I still think it's a religion of fear. And your father is afraid in a way. Not just for you, but for himself as well. I've told him to go to church, if that's what he wants. He doesn't go. He just worries about it. So read the book, if you want. Decide for yourself."

A story I heard when I was about thirty shone some light on the religious push and pull in my family. My father and his brother were sons of an Irish Catholic mother, a widow for many years. Both sons had married outside the faith. My grandmother made it widely known that their apostasy would be her cross to bear for the rest of her life, which proved to be a long time. In the nursing home at age ninety-two, she still bemoaned their marriages. I seldom saw her, because she lived in Ohio. This was just fine with me, because I thought her haughty and difficult. Even my father, who sent money to his brother for her support, didn't seem eager to get closer to her.

She had moved to the nursing home five years before, following a showdown at my uncle's house, where she'd been living. Here's the report that came to me. In keeping with her usual routine, she had settled down one afternoon for a double bourbon on the rocks. My uncle's two teenaged children were listening to music nearby. My grandmother chose the moment to vent again about the poor judgment of her sons.

"Your mother is going to Hell," she announced to the children. Like one of the Greek Furies, she cursed them. "She's a whore who's going to burn. And you will, too, if you don't change your ways."

Stunned, they looked at one another. While they were used to her mean-spirited outbursts, this went beyond her past ranting. They had no response.

But their mother did. She entered the room just as their grandmother returned to her drink.

"How dare you speak to my children that way?" she demanded. "Is this what we get for feeding you, giving you a place to live, for caring for you? You rotten old ingrate. I've had it with you."

My grandmother, however, was emboldened by her faith. God, she blazed, was on her side. It was better the children know the truth. Her son had sinned in marrying as he did. On and on. My uncle, drawn in by the raised voices, received his wife's ultimatum: Either this bitter old woman leaves, or I do.

In a few days, my grandmother was in the home. Over the next few years, that's where she stayed except for brief, carefully controlled holiday visits to my aunt and uncle. My uncle, however, went to see her almost every day. In phone calls to my father, he reported her continuing bitterness. And he told of her several escapes from the home—how he'd tracked her down a block or two from the property. It was bourbon and meanness that kept her going, the brothers decided.

Later, when I was visiting my parents in Florida, my father, who was then about sixty-five, called his mother on Mother's Day. After his cheerful greeting, he stood head down at the phone, from which her raspy, accusatory voice could be heard. I couldn't make out what she was saying, but from my father's submissive responses, I gathered she was chewing him out about something. Sixty-five and still being excoriated by his mother. A wayward son still wallowing in sin.

Ten years later, my father returned to the Church. He joined a small congregation at St. Michael's. My mother reported that he seemed to find some comfort there. But he wanted more. On one of my visits, she told me that he wanted them to renew their vows—to be married again, this time at St. Michael's as Catholics. She was angry.

"You'd think almost fifty years of marriage would satisfy him. Was that for nothing? Sometimes, I can't stand this stuff. Was his bitchy mother an example of what he wants?"

On my next visit, five months later, she surprised me, telling me she would probably do it, although it would mean some classes with teachings she abhorred.

Shaking her head, she said, "But, if it will bring your father peace, I'll guess I could do it."

After dinner, as I was putting my bag into the car, my father came to my side.

"Son," he said, "I've got some great news. Over the years, I think your mother has given a lot of thought to Catholicism. And she's found that there's a lot to it. In fact, we're going to get married again at St. Michael's. Father William will give us some instruction before the wedding. This will be great for us."

They were married again. After all those years, my father was free of a burden—marrying outside the faith. And my mother had taken on a burden of love.

When I returned to the hospital with my father, my mother was sleeping. But she sensed our presence and slowly opened her eyes, still dark brown, still lit from within. She spoke softly, just above a whisper. Long periods of silence punctuated our conversation about mundane matters. No one seemed to know quite what to say. My father held her hand. I placed my hand lightly on her ankle.

When she again fell asleep, I looked at my father. Tears washed his face, and he was trembling.

"Come on, Dad, let's go home while she sleeps." I whispered. "We can come back tomorrow . . . or again tonight, if you want."

He nodded. I helped him up and guided him out toward the parking lot. At the exit, we were intercepted by a young physician, who introduced himself as my mother's surgeon. Surgeon? I wondered. For what?

The surgeon explained that my mother had an abscess on her leg. She needed minor surgery to clear it up. Otherwise the infection might spread. My father was alarmed. I was incensed. Why, I demanded, would you operate on a woman who has refused treatment for terminal cancer and is dying now? While the surgeon continued on about risks and benefits and protocol, I pushed past him with my father in tow. I felt we were escaping a bad horror movie.

At home, my father, who had been so strong and vigorous all his life, faltered. He didn't know what to do or say. He hardly knew what to think. Late in the afternoon, he finally mustered the energy to go to church. He returned with an idea: that Father William might visit my mother in the hospital. She was, after all, a Catholic, he said.

I hesitated. Then I said, "Let's think about it, Dad. Maybe we can ask her what she wants." I stopped short of mentioning last rites, but I knew the ritual was on his mind.

My father began to protest, but his voice trailed away. "I just want to make sure . . ." Then silently he shook his head.

"Get some rest, Dad. We'll go back for a short visit tonight," I said. But I wondered which need was greater: to prevent the encroachment of religiosity on my mother's final hours or to accede to my father's need for the priest to bless her.

The sun had set when we again flanked her bed. Husband by her head; son by her feet—no priest. Her irregular breathing hardly moved the covering sheet. Her eyes were closed. When I squeezed her ankle, she made no response. We sat there, for minutes or hours. In that sterile place of tubes and machines, she died with only our hands laid upon her. Later, in my own hospital stay, I would learn how much touch can mean.

As I looked at her lying so still, I thought of her idea of a wonderful life. The Depression, the war, breast cancer, even becoming a Catholic. Looking back, she had let all that go. She had seen only the best. For me her death was a teaching.

A week later, as I was gathering up some things from her bedroom, I came across a poem she had copied onto several index cards. I'd seen the poem in various forms before. Don't stand at my grave and cry, her version said. I'm not there. I did not die.

I decided that with the text, my mother had prepared her own last rites. I read it silently several times. Then I read it once aloud . . .

> I am the thousand winds that blow,
> I am the diamond glints in snow,
> I am the sunlight on ripened grain,
> I am the gentle autumn rain . . .

As I spoke the lines, I looked out the window. Small palm trees were waving in the breeze. I heard my father moving about in the other room. Ordinary happenings from which my mother was gone. A surge of sadness choked me. But I continued my reading. I could hear her admonition.

> Do not stand at my grave and cry;
> I am not there. I did not die.

THE WAR HERO DEPARTS

Full fathom five thy father lies,
Of his bones are coral made,
Those are pearls that were his eyes.
Nothing of him that doth fade
But doth suffer a sea change
Into something rich and strange.
—*Shakespeare*

There he stands poolside with a long-handled net and a beer on a table conveniently nearby. It is almost noon. The pool is enclosed in screens, so it's not leaves or other detritus from the trees or surrounding golf course that calls for my father's attention. Small lizards somehow find ways to get into the cage that encloses the pool and patio. He's on a mission to rescue the occasional stray that has fallen into the pool. Those he skims out, living and dead, he tosses onto the bushes by the pool with an expert twist of the net.

The beer is an ever-present adjunct to his lizard hunting. It is, I know, his way of numbing the pain arising from the residual shrapnel in his leg. There he stands under dappled Florida sunlight, surrounded by swatches of color, with music from his radio softly playing. Fifty years removed from the hell of combat. But each day, the pain in his leg brings him back to that time. And I wonder how much his heart is pained by that recollection.

While I was in college, my parents moved to Connecticut when my father was promoted to manage the New York City office of the International Silver Company. Over the years, Flash, the dynamic salesman of silver tableware, had garnered an enviable reputation throughout the organization. Now management wanted him to revitalize their important, but flagging, New York enterprise. So he traded his car for a promotion and daily train rides in and out of the city.

The work in the city was quite an undertaking. His tales of work life suggested the vigor he brought to the job. On his knees praying about a host of esoteric subjects with a major buyer, buying a second order of lamb chops for a customer whose dog "so enjoyed them," and an early morning foray to the city to personally buy several sets of International tableware being sold at a discount and thereby defend the product's price.

He was Flash again when he regaled us with such stories. But by now, I knew that with my father, feelings and actions could quickly change. Still, my parents seemed to enjoy their new situation. He was home each night and had time to enter into the social life of their neighborhood, where trains in and out of the city shaped the rhythm of life.

In a couple of years, I learned of his intent to move to Florida. First, a scouting trip—a vacation my parents took to escape some of the oppressive winter of the Northeast. They returned with photos and the usual motley collection of souvenirs. My father, however, held one out as special. It was an aerial photograph of an orange grove on which were outlined plots where houses were to be built.

When I next saw my parents, one of those plots had an X marked through it. They had committed to moving to Florida. My father was excited and enthusiastic. He had arranged with his company to cover a territory centered on Sarasota, where they would be living. Easier travel and lots of sunshine. My mother was less eager to move. She felt tied to the Northeast. She would miss its rough edges. But my father so wanted the move that she accepted the change.

So they built their retirement home, a modest house with a pool on the edge of a golf course. In all, the development was more pleasant and attractive than what I had imagined when I first saw the marked-up photograph two years before. My mother had occasional urges to return to the Northeast, but these were assuaged in part by the arrival in the neighborhood of several couples with whom my parents had long been close. My parents lived there happily until my mother died.

So there he was, beer in hand, scouring the pool for

lizards. Had it been a month earlier, she would have been sitting just inside working on a crossword puzzle. But today, her usual chair was empty. In accordance with her wishes, her ashes had been scattered over the Florida Gulf.

It hadn't worked out the way my mother had wanted—for him to die first. As she had warned me, he didn't know how much he depended on her. He didn't know that she was the stronger and could abide the loss better than he. What to do with my father now that my mother was no more?

He was well settled in their home, but my mother had been right. Once she was gone, he quickly became uncertain about his path in life. Trips to the store that had been so easy made him anxious. He fretted over household tasks that had come as second nature to him. As I watched him poke idly at the water, it became clear to me that he could not stay there on his own. It was as if my mother's death had pulled a plug, and his vitality was draining away. In conversation, he was much my father—even showing brief glimpses of Flash—but in making decisions, he faltered. I couldn't leave him there alone, and I couldn't bear the prospect of him in an assisted living facility so far away. So I decided to bring him to Houston, where I could keep close watch on him.

The problem was that his view of his capabilities differed greatly from mine. First, he contended he could live alone in Florida. In a few days, however, he had modified his view. He could use a little help. The argument that carried the day centered on family. My wife and I lived in Houston with two of his grandchildren. With Helen gone, his place now was with us. So we settled. He would move to his own place in Houston. Hence began a series of deceptions that continued until he died.

The proceeds from the sale of his house were modest, and in a mean-spirited maneuver, his company had slashed his pension. He had been their most productive salesman, commanding a good salary with substantial commissions when he headed their office in New York City. When he asked to move to Florida a few years before retirement, they had accommodated him with territory he could handle in a reprise of his early act as traveling salesman. Naturally, they couldn't pay him what they would for the New York City job. Fair enough, my father said. It would only be for a couple of years.

What the company failed to mention was that his pension would be based on his average compensation over his last two years with the company. When his first check arrived, substantially less than expected, he learned of this hard-hearted arithmetic. All those years of service to the company, and this reward. Rummaging through some papers in a desk drawer, I found an explanation of benefits that would have been a warning, but no evidence that my father had ever looked at it. And no one, he said, had mentioned this during discussions of his moving to Florida.

Still, he was insistent that he pay his way. Our family never put our burdens on others. I told him that, for convenience, I would handle his banking account. I rented an apartment in the Forum, an upscale assisted-living facility that was well beyond his means. And for the first time in so many years, I lied to my father. For several years, until his death, to allay his fears, I told him that I had struck a deal with the owner that brought the price within his reach. Had he known that I was paying his rent, I think he would have been miserable.

To ease the transition, I had furniture from home moved to furnish his new quarters. He insisted on bringing his car. Perhaps he imagined that driving in Houston was like driving in Sarasota. I was not able to persuade him to sell his car. Now that I am mostly housebound myself, I can understand the importance of a car as a vehicle to freedom. Giving up a car is admitting a defeat from which there will be no recovery.

So the car came to Houston to be parked in the garage at the Forum. Until one day, when I received a call from the management. My father had been found by security guards in the Galleria, a shopping mall near his building. He couldn't find his way out of the garage and couldn't remember his address. Fortunately, the parking permit in his car had the address of the Forum. A few days later, he grudgingly allowed me to sell his car.

And so it went. I gave him a fish tank with a variety of bright, active tropicals. Feeding instructions were simple. A small amount of food sprinkled over the surface twice each day. Often, however, when I visited, I found the tank clouded from too many feedings. The murky water was a sad indicator of my father's fading away. But when his granddaughters visited, he showed his old charm and wit. And when I visited alone, Flash often emerged, although the story he told may have been one he had told the day before. He still told it well.

With the furniture from Florida, the apartment at the Forum was very attractive and comfortable. And a number of residents had taken an interest in my father. He told me that he was frequently invited to join one group or another for meals. Most of these were women, he said. I was happy for him. But he was wary. Once, clasping my arm, he looked directly at me. "Listen, son. I'm not doing anything with them. You understand."

I understood. Often, he told me how he talked to Helen.

I last saw my father at the Veteran's Hospital in Houston. For a week or so, he'd been having some pains in his stomach. I'd scheduled him for a visit to his doctor. But that night, he had called for help at the Forum, and they had called me. As he passed by on a stretcher into an exam room, he lifted his head a bit and called to me, "Hey, son." Only minutes later, in that room, Flash, the War Hero, left the field forever.

I had his ashes scattered over the Florida Gulf where he could be with Helen again.

SEEING AND SEEING AGAIN

> A person's life consists of a collection of events,
> the last of which could also change the meaning
> of the whole, not because it counts more than the
> previous ones but because once they are included
> in a life, events are arranged in an order that is not
> chronological but, rather, corresponds to an inner
> architecture.
>
> —*Italo Calvino*

A few years before returning to my hometown for
my high school reunion, I was rummaging through
my motley collection of family artifacts. In the bottom
of a box of my mother's things, I came upon a folder I
hadn't seen before. In it several prints had been slipped

between some old documents. I recognized a number of the pictures as George's work. I remembered the places pictured in all but one. In that one, a dilapidated barn, seen from across a field of tall dry grass, stands forlornly against a wooded backdrop. The door of the barn is ajar, revealing a deeply shadowed inside. A broken window confirms interior darkness. Many times, I've studied the rough exterior and the rusted tools that lie before it. I've devoted myself to the roof with its loose shingles and apparent holes. Now I remember being there. But I never visited the barn. I've just looked at the picture so often, I feel I know what lies behind those walls. Sometimes I sense that, defying natural law, something will emerge from within. But unlike cloud watching, patient waiting and looking haven't helped.

My uncle was the photographer, but over the years, he became for me the subject of imagined photos. Where I once only saw a lonely, dilapidated barn, I now see him. When in memory, I follow my father and my uncle on their walk along that tree-roofed street so long ago, I find it remarkable that they connected as they did. For my uncle, the walk along Sherman Avenue must often have been shadowed not just by the trees, but by doubts about his life and future as well. Perhaps he felt it determined that he would always walk this street to his mother's house, and another path, which he had vaguely hoped to follow, but had been unable to find, would never be open to him. Early on, it had been clear that he was smart, a "brain" he had often been called, so it was no surprise that now he was an actuary. But it had been equally clear that he was a bit odd. When his interest was stirred, as it had been earlier that afternoon long ago, he could find something to offer, particularly on fishing and photography, about which he could hold forth engagingly. While he was an inveterate banterer, he might suddenly become wary of a topic which to others seemed uncontroversial, even mundane, yet to him presaged danger. Then if he couldn't divert the conversation, fidgeting, coughing, with his red face more reddened, he would mumble a few words, excusing himself to attend to some important but unspecified matter.

Perhaps it was the same when my uncle tried to talk to himself about his future. Unease might quickly grant him some excuse to flee to a more congenial subject, which suddenly seemed particularly pressing. Had it not been for his family's constant course corrections, he would not have found his way to college, where his aptitude for mathematics and logic secured more than decent success in the classroom. His cautious amiability, abetted by the unflagging efforts of his older brother, who was a year ahead at the same college, and a sister, my mother, at a women's college nearby, created a social life that sputtered but never flamed.

At graduation, he knew probability and statistics, but he took few chances in life. Despite his success in the classroom, he found himself still unlearned in making sense of his life, so he returned, to his hometown, and to his childhood house—to his past. After almost a year, nudged by his family, he more or less stumbled into the actuarial position at the insurance company. In the years that followed, when occasional views of a different tomorrow arose or were thrust upon him by one of the dwindling few concerned that he should make more of himself, a jumble of thoughts and feelings arose to obstruct his vision, and another imagined future was irrevocably lost.

As I child I knew none of this, of course. Uncle George amply fulfilled my father's charge—to watch over, entertain, and nurture me in his absence. My writing and repeated returns to the past helped me to a new, unsettling understanding.

And the folder held some other prints. One is the picture of my father, Flash, the War Hero, standing alone by the tank in the rubble-strewn street of that foreign town. In another, still in uniform, my father reaches happily to clutch my mother on the glad day of his homecoming. But there are several more—horrific pictures of death. These must be the prints George snatched up when I discovered the War Hero. Jumbled corpses in a roadside ditch. A woman with a long skirt lying with her arm across the chest of a young girl, who stares blankly at the sky. Bodies scattered like broken, cast-away dolls. Finally, two soldiers face down in watery ground, their legs entangled in barbed wire. Awful, intimate pictures of death. My father needed no prints to remember the horrors of war. Combat seared these images and many others on his heart.

Sometimes the change in our memory can be sudden, like one of those optical illusions, say a drawing of a duck that on second glance reveals a rabbit. In the same collection, I found a snapshot which I'd never seen before. It showed me my mother in a new way. I saw that she had been beautiful. It was not that she was conventionally pretty, although she would certainly have been considered quite attractive. The way she stood, slender and alert, added ineffably to her appeal. Although the picture is now more than eighty years old, her eyes still seem to sparkle. Her energy still emanates from them. She was said to have many good qualities—honesty, industry, compassion, for example. But I never heard anyone, not even my father, say she was beautiful. Yet he couldn't have detected these qualities during that first dinner on Sherman Avenue. He must have been enthralled by her beauty and intelligence.

When I entered my teens and first puzzled over the attractions of women, I occasionally wondered why my father, a dashing war hero, had fallen for her. By then, of course, she was my mother, not the striking girl in the picture. Why was I so surprised by that photo? Largely, I think, because of the ways in which she directed her energies. And because she paid little attention to her looks. She chose her clothes for comfort, in keeping with her work around the house. With a few quick brushes she arranged her hair. When a social occasion was in the offing, she pinched her cheeks with coloring from her lipstick. If she saw me watching her, she'd say, "Rouge," and laugh. In a way, she taught me how to see her. But some years later, memory has shown her to me in a much different way.

Pictures, George, Helen, and Flash, interleaved. A mixture of love and loss settles on me whenever I look at them. They're not images in the clouds. They're not in stately motion to new, perhaps happier configurations.

Now that digital images are so malleable, we are less inclined to credit their testimony. But these were fixed by life's developing fluids and etched on the yellowing paper of the past. They were printed before cameras became computers and have been frozen in space and time for decades. Perhaps they are more trustworthy. Still, by themselves they explain nothing. They did, however, lay a claim on me to ponder their meaning, which has shifted and deepened with time. Here in the present, the prints, like the iron gate before my grandmother's house, create a portal to the past. The same is true of my father's medals. Looking long at the artifacts has changed my recollections of the people they represent and my life with them.

I walked from my grandmother's house to the home my parents built. There, I stood beneath the maple tree grown grand in the years since my departure. Its leaves quivered in the light autumn breeze. Green turning to red and orange, they would soon change to brown. Once in a while, a leaf detached itself from a branch and spiraled slowly down, joining a rough circle of colors that was forming around me. Soon, the rakes would be out again to create another invitation to a happy childhood.

YELLOWED PAGES

Now, eight years after my reunion, I turn to a folder that lies on my desk between my father's medals and my uncle's photographs. In it are sketches and scribbled notes. It's unusual for me to have such a collection, because I've never dealt well with paper. Lists of things to do, books to read, people to see—I make them, but ignore or quickly lose them. Now lots more paper comes my way: instructions from physicians and nurses, lab reports, medication lists, hospital bills, insurance filings, solicitations. I let most of it pass by, but I've saved these few pages in a folder between the other two artifacts.

Here is one page, which, if you could see it, you might at first take for a child's drawing, perhaps a tree barren but for a few leaves. Moving closer, however, you would see that the leaves are numbers jotted alongside the penciled branches. A doctor, not a child, made the cryptic sketch as he told me about the management of acute myeloblastic leukemia, a disease that had suddenly become mine. The tree is a kind of code I have long understood, but lately often wished I'd never learned. This tree is not one of the sheltering elms of Sherman Avenue. The sketch encodes a message about a grim destroyer skulking in my blood. Branches show paths the disease might take; numbers, the chances branches will be chosen. Branches and chances together form a kind of map of my future. The skeletal tree marks the entrance to a gloomy place, where most numbers incline paths to dour dead ends. In Homer, a new day comes with rosy-fingered Dawn rising from her couch to spread light on the world. Yet dark clouds of doom can gather, even in a day that begins brightly. As she did to my father and my uncle, she now brings me days fraught with uncertainty and peril.

Also in the folder I come on a yellowed newspaper page from four decades ago in which I am pictured with three physicians standing before a blackboard, where leafless trees have been drawn like the one my hematologist sketched for me. The picture and the accompanying article appeared several years after I had begun research in artificial intelligence with the ambition to create a program that would perform as well as expert clinicians do. But how? The mental processes of physicians seemed mysterious. Watching physicians work revealed little about how they thought. They themselves generally attributed their skills to an inexplicable intuition, a product of long experience. Forty years ago, intuition lay outside the realm of computing, and it still does today.

So my physician colleagues and I cast an "understanding" of aspects of medicine in numbers—probabilities and so-called utilities or values—that allowed reasoning by calculation, which suited the computer well. In a surprise to many physicians, the program matched their decision-making in a number of medical areas. Two different ways of thinking—intuitive and computational—arrived at the same conclusions. This success had attracted the attention of the newspaper. It was easy for the writer of the article to anthropomorphize the program, to attribute judgment to it, to see it reflecting on alternative hypotheses. Its ways, however, were mechanistic, devoid of such faculties. It could "know" something, in this case the cause of a constellation of symptoms, without knowing or caring anything about it. That early work came quickly to mind when I first learned of my medical situation. In our digital age, we are connected to everything; knowing without understanding has become the fashion, not just among computers, but among people as well, and it has become easy to claim for ourselves more knowledge than we actually possess.

During the decade following the implementation of my program, I encouraged physicians to use its methodical ways, called decision analysis, to bolster their reasoning in certain clinical situations. Many did, and in the following years, decision analysis proved helpful for a variety of diagnostic and therapeutic problems. One of its putative virtues is the separation of probabilities of outcomes and the values placed on them. The physician is the likely authority on the former; the patient, on the latter. In difficult cases, therefore, decision analysis may improve communication and collaboration. It requires, however, that the implicit be made explicit. Probabilities that at first may be only feelings must be written down, and explicit assessments of potential consequences have to be made. Early on, for every physician who found value in decision analysis, I encountered another who found it an alien way of thinking about patient care. The rumpled pages on my desk take me back to that discomfort. I see in the sketches places where tensions between numbers and feelings pulled on my physicians—and tugged on me as well. At those points, I scoured the Internet, and then I finally took my place in the older garden of memory and imagination.

I had thought to apply decision analysis to the choices before me: chemotherapy, stem cell transplantation, or in the worst case, palliative care. I would fill that stark white space with a decision tree derived from conversations with my physicians and self-guided tours of the Eden of everything. Today, however, that space is largely unmarked, and I have added nothing to the notes. Looking back, I imagine my physicians standing with me peering into that emptiness, speculating on what I would find should I venture in, warning of hidden dangers, or declaring the path I should take. But they were not decision analysts. On several occasions, I quizzed them about probabilities. Were there aspects of my case that might call for an adjustment of the odds of various outcomes? Several answered roughly like this: "The probabilities, the odds, are just numbers. Each patient is unique. You'll have a relapse or you won't." In their unwillingness to apply "statistics" to my particular case, I heard echoes of the voices of physicians from decades ago for whom the probabilities that lived in journal reports were only loosely related to those in patient care.

Of course, my doctors, and those from earlier years, recognized the uncertainty of the clinical setting; they dealt with it every day, but they seemed reluctant to blend general probabilities from various studies with their knowledge of particular patients. Such a calculus was not part of their lore. Instead, they seemed more like members of a learned and priestly class, all wanting the best for me, but sometimes at odds in their reading of omens and foretelling of consequences.

At the time, I was reading Herodotus, a fifth-century Greek called the first historian. He told of the oracles of ancient Greece, women who served as mediums through whom mortals could communicate with the gods. The most prominent oracle was the Pythia, priestess of Apollo at his temple at Delphi. She answered questions from kings, statesmen, and even philosophers on personal matters as well as those of great import such as governance, disease, and even war. To access the divine, the Pythia burned sacred laurel leaves in the innermost recesses of the temple, where fumes from underground deepened her trance. Devotees attending her translated her pronouncements, which would otherwise have been unintelligible. The Pythia was notorious for ambiguous answers whose true import would be realized only in hindsight. Herodotus writes that King Croesus of Lydia consulted her before attacking Persia. "If you do, you will destroy a great empire," declaimed the oracle.

Taking this as a favorable response, Croesus attacked, but the great empire that was destroyed proved to be his own.

Imagine for a moment a minor revolt at Apollo's temple. The tide of inquiry has been rising, and the temple attendants, who by now consider themselves well-versed in the sayings of the Pythia, begin offering counsels of their own. Seeing the opportunity for a respite from her wearying chores, or perhaps piqued by her loss of prominence, the Pythia retreats deep into her cave, leaving her attendants to deal with the suppliants as best they can. As the attendants step forward there is greater access to prophecy, but this increase of access leads to greater ambiguity and often deeper dissatisfaction.

Technology has fomented its own rebellion, the revolt of the masses foreseen a century ago by Ortega y Gasset, in which the many have asserted their rights over activities for which special learning and preparation had previously been thought indispensable. Radical egalitarianism now holds sway on the Internet, where everyone is a potential publisher, commentator, or broadcaster, and every analysis, critique, or rendition is but a mouse click away. For more than two centuries, the editors of the *Encyclopedia Britannica* proclaimed it one of the most trusted sources of information on "almost every topic imaginable." Its authority stemmed from their judicious choice of subjects, careful selection of experts, and emphasis on quality control. Now *Britannica* has been pushed aside by Wikipedia, the encyclopedia of the masses, for the masses. Wikipedia encompasses millions of articles about a bewildering array of subjects. Each article is malleable and hence provisional; readers can edit, amend, and expand it dynamically. Loosely put, Wikipedia has vested authority in the wisdom of the crowd, trusting the watchful many to detect misstatements, errors, and biases, and to weed them out quickly. Some doubt the trustworthiness of Wikipedia, but not the many millions who turn to it first for information about a broad range of subjects.

Herodotus was no armchair historian inspired by the divine. He was an inveterate traveler who spent most of his life wandering Persian domains, including Egypt, Babylon, many Greek islands, the lands bordering the Black Sea and the Danube River. In his travels, he saw many wonders and heard of many more. He observed exotic peoples and places and listened to legends, folk tales, and myths as well as contemporary reports regarding customs and happenings. To each of these sources he assigned roughly equal importance. While he was concerned with the conflict between the Greeks and Persians, he was also attracted to gossip, particularly when it supported a moral lesson he wished to teach. His work cobbled together geography, mythology, aspects of anthropology, and liberal borrowing from the work of others, notably Homer. His history is entertaining, informative, fascinating, true, and false. No wonder. He was in a rush with so many places to see, so little time, and so much to assimilate.

The stubborn physicality of our ordinary lives no longer limits the range of our travel. Without leaving my hospital room, I could effortlessly wander the burgeoning Eden of everything. The Internet, which in its early years was said to be an information highway, has

proved a far grander thoroughfare than was then foreseen. As anticipated in its early days, we now frequent
stores of information along its electronic pathways, although the scope and scale of these resources far exceed
those previously imagined. Unforeseen was an Internet
teeming with social interaction, and unanticipated was
the proliferation of digital devices that at work, home,
and play give us continuous access to this parallel world
within which are increasingly found the tracks of modern life.

The number and variety of Internet oracles is aston-
ishing. Who doesn't seek them out for facts and advice
about a range of topics and for connections with friends
and family spread far and wide? Like Herodotus, we
have so much to assimilate and so little time. So we
often learn just enough just in time for our purposes.
What we know is often hastily improvised from bits and
pieces of technologically mediated experiences. In the
rush of our lives, we may seize on eclectic and uncertain offerings as though they embodied revealed truth.

There are many Internet oracles eager to answer my
questions, ease my uncertainties, and give me guidance,
many who would interpret omens regarding my disease. While the Pythia was inspired by Apollo, most of
my Internet oracles bestow the mantle of authority on
themselves as a consequence of an illness or an acquaintance with someone who has suffered some form of leukemia. Statistics that might have informed my choices
were readily at hand, but most had been gleaned from
small numbers of patients who probably differed from
me in significant, but unrecorded ways. The patchwork
of numbers, anecdotes, and impressions reminded me

of a fabulous account by the ancient historian. Gossip, stories, eyewitness accounts, and false reports swirled together to form what would pass for knowledge. So it wasn't surprising that the management of my case was controversial.

A WALK IN THE WOODS
WITH PROUST

> People do not die for us immediately, but remain bathed in a sort of aura of life which bears no relation to true immortality but through which they continue to occupy our thoughts in the same way as when they were alive. It is as though they were traveling abroad.
>
> —*Marcel Proust*

For more than seven years, I've lived in the shadow of those leafless trees. Early on, they cast a darkness over my life, which I had no ready light to dispel. But there was not much time for investigation. In a matter of days, I was settled in a sterile hospital room under the care of a team of physicians. A single bed and a couple of nondescript chairs. No rug, just an overhead TV set and a picture on one wall that had likely been painted by a machine. I was attached to another machine that dripped toxic chemicals into my arm day and night.

There are few ways to fend off boredom during an extended hospital stay. My modest exercise program consisted of circuits of the ward maneuvering a pole with several IV bags. A small built-in desk provided a compact workspace. My computer allowed me to enter the electronic world where so much of today's life transpires. A chair with a lamp and side table served as my library nook.

After work and exercise, I had ample time for reading. Friends contributed mystery novels, and I chose some books I'd pushed aside in the rush of the outside world. I renewed acquaintances with Cervantes, Tolstoy, and Proust. They were gateways to other times and places.

Proust ushered me into nineteenth-century French society, a far remove from my current surroundings. Reading the first volume of *Remembrance of Things Past*, however, I felt some unease. Not because six more volumes lay ahead, but because Marcel, Proust's alter ego, is a whiner. In the midst of lofty reflections on art, love, imagination, and life, he descends into complaining. Marcel grumbled about drafts, light, and even the position of his bed. Egotistical, narcissistic, vain—and what a hypochondriac he was. All his life, Proust himself was dogged by a variety of real and imagined ailments. His fear of sickness could become morbidly pronounced. In his later years, even certain smells terrified him. At the end, he lived in a cork-lined room to suppress noises from outside, which he also found very unnerving. Hard to imagine that a self-absorbed man who cowered before a world rife with imagined dangers could bolster my spirits in the face of a real and deadly disease.

But in the second volume, in his heightened sensitivity to illness, he suggested some new ways for me to think about the path that lay ahead. In recalling his grandmother's illness, he became not just my entertainment and distraction, but my companion. Although he often spoke metaphorically, what he conveyed seemed to apply to my situation.

"You don't live alone," he said as we started out on our walk together. You're chained to your body, a being from another realm that doesn't care a whit about you. Disease arises from the anger of that being.

I first found this an odd thought, but soon saw what he meant. In the minor aches, pains and illnesses of everyday life, my body seldom behaved as I wanted. But when ailments faded, so did my awareness of its alien nature. Now it was very angry, as Proust would have it. Its indifference to my wishes and supplications was clear—and deeply unsettling. Neither bargaining nor pleading would rid me of leukemia. My hope lay in the knowledge and skills of my doctors, who would accompany me on my journey.

Proust, however, didn't hold doctors in high esteem. His grandmother's recent death had done nothing to improve his opinion of them. Those who attended her had few insights into her illness and even fewer ways to relieve it. What Proust called emissaries from her body's realm delivered messages coded in temperature, blood, skin, and vital capacities. Had they been able to read these, her physicians might have known if her body's anger was unyielding or might soon be stilled. But, alas, Proust said, they really couldn't understand the language of the body.

Well, I thought, you're recalling medicine near the end of the nineteenth century when the practice was hardly scientific. Look around. The equipment in my room testifies to remarkable progress since your grandmother's day. My doctors understand much more of what my body is saying. I've had countless blood tests. I've undergone x-rays, scans and bone marrow biopsies. What my doctors know about my leukemia would have been a wonder to their predecessors. So your description of medicine seems quaint.

Furthermore, experience and experimentation have transmuted medical practice for many diseases, including some insidious and vicious ones. Guidelines and standards of care have supplanted idiosyncratic approaches to treatment. Even we patients feel a smug superiority to your physicians of a century ago. In your grandmother's case, one prescribed a milk diet; another, fresh air and willful disregard of symptoms; and a third, complete bed rest. What kind of medicine was that?

My physicians set my initial course in accord with a widely accepted protocol. The route would be arduous and risky, but science could be expected to illuminate the way. For a week, they dripped potent compounds with exotic names such as idarubicin and cytarabine into my veins. Again invoking metaphor, Proust would characterize these drugs as creatures not content to question the body, but determined to command it. They reconnoitered the ground, seeking opportunities for combat. In my case, their intent was to obliterate bone marrow, the den in which the leukemia lurked. They were vicious mercenaries unconcerned with collateral damage: nausea, vomiting, headaches, skin rashes, swelling, and other consequences of their mayhem.

My doctors unleashed the drugs in the hope that my bone marrow, reborn from the devastation wrought by these chemical warriors, would be free of disease. A hope it was, because even as they infused me, they knew that the likelihood of victory was small. Had they not told me this, I could have easily found such an assessment on the Internet. Yet in the weeks that followed, blood tests and bone marrow biopsies were promising. No evidence of leukemia. Maybe with my doctors as guides, I was on a path out of darkness.

After several months, however, my situation turned bleak. Leukemia had smoldered in the ruined bone marrow and was again on the advance. Statistics that might have guided my doctors had been gleaned from small numbers of patients who probably differed from me in significant, but unrecorded ways. The patchwork of numbers, anecdotes, and impressions couldn't be read with certainty. As it did for those who attended Proust's grandmother, a hazy picture of the terrain stirred doubt as to how best to proceed.

Had the first attack on my disease then been for naught? Or worse?

Back in my hospital room, Proust seemed to argue that despite the paraphernalia surrounding me little had changed from his grandmother's time. Blows aimed at the evil inside her were always wide of the mark. The pain she suffered returned no benefit. The ferocious beast that had been the target had just been grazed. Even more enraged, it was hastening the moment when it would devour her.

In my case, the leukemia cells that had survived the initial onslaught, by a perverse Darwinian selection, were likely to be more virulent, more malevolent than their predecessors. Like Proust's beast, they would be angrier. I had joined the ranks of those who suffered but were not healed: surgery hadn't removed all the offending tissue; radiation hadn't eliminated all the malignant cells; chemotherapy hadn't repressed the disease. We were all pushed deeper into murkiness to confront the anger of the body, which had likely increased.

My hematologist had little patience with Proust, whose view he deemed "uncharitable." Chemotherapy, he said, had stalled the advance of leukemia, if only for a few months. That he considered this an accomplishment reflected his dour view of my prognosis. Sadly, I understood his assessment.

At the time I was sixty-nine years old. Not many years before, death would have certainly loomed. Other than palliative care, more chemotherapy would have been deemed my only recourse, and a poor one at that. Recent advances in medicine, however, have made stem cell transplantation an option for older leukemia patients. The donor cells may create a new bone marrow that is free of leukemia.

This intervention would be risky. I would need additional debilitating chemotherapy in order to destroy my bone marrow again. Then stem cells from a stranger could build a new immune system. The donor cells, however, are hostile to what they sense as foreign. They generally induce what is known as graft-versus-host disease (GVHD), which is thought to have an anti-leukemic effect. Because all my body would be foreign to the new immune system, my heart, lung, liver, skin, and eyes would be potential targets for its hostility. The virulence of its attacks might be controlled by immunosuppressive drugs. If not, GVHD would likely prove as deadly as the leukemia it was intended to combat.

Neither chemotherapy nor transplantation offered substantial hope. My doctors found themselves beyond the surety of scientific medicine. Intuition, feelings, hunches, and perhaps wishes came into play. Looking back, I imagine them ruminating on the dangers that lay ahead and pondering the path I should take. They seemed like members of a learned, priestly class, all wanting the best for me, but sometimes at odds in their reading of omens and foretelling of consequences. Some concluded that chemotherapy, despite its meager prospects, offered the better choice; others settled on stem cell transplantation; and one would only opine, in what was no news to me, that it was "a tough decision."

Proust spoke up here not about what my choice should be, but about making it. "Our final decisions," he said, "are made in a state of mind that is not going to last." Guesses often prove wrong, and promises go unfulfilled. But choices must be made. Recognizing that later days might cast my decision in a different light, I opted for a stem cell transplant, and on we went.

Chemotherapy again destroyed my bone marrow. But the transplant was uneventful: a short infusion of donor cells followed by a month in the hospital while a new immune system took up residence. Six months later, however, leukemia again returned. Perhaps, my doctors thought, an influx of donor T-cells might stymie its resurgence. No, the disease continued its advance. I was now well off the path, likely to be permanently lost among dark trees unreached by the light of science.

Another transplant with cells from a different donor offered a last small hope. In this dreary place, Proust had sobering advice for managing expectations. "Medicine," he said, "is a compendium of the successive and contradictory mistakes of its practitioners." Scientific truth upon which the wisest now rely will in years to come be recognized as error. To believe in medicine, therefore, would be the height of folly. No, to choose not to believe in it would be a greater folly still, for it is from many errors that a few truths emerge.

The remarkable trappings around my hospital bed of modern medicine suggested that rationality holds sway over the medical realm. But Proust was right. A part of medicine is always on the verge between certainty and mystery. Science moves the boundary only to reveal new uncertainties. Physicians must probe, grope, invent explanations, and employ unproven strategies. They study the latest journals, seeking reports of newly won truths about the body. I live today because of emergent truths, which even when uncertainty and doubt loom, give physicians last chances, if not sure defenses against leukemia.

Patients may seek truth elsewhere. Proust said, "Illness is the doctor to whom we pay most heed; to kindness, to knowledge, we make promise only; pain we obey." Some of my pain was of the body, but like his, more was of the spirit. He added that we discover wisdom only after a journey that no one can take for us—or spare us. My doctors might heal my body, but only I could heal the pain of my heart. I thought of my parents and their encounters with death. I thought of the Greek heroes. I thought of what it meant to be heroic. I parted from Proust with a promise to join him again after I had taken my walk alone.

After my second transplant, pneumonia brought me back to the hospital. A week in the intensive care unit followed by a month of recovery. Several weeks into my stay, a soft knock on my door preceded the cautious entry of a slender young man. A minister had come to offer me comfort in "my situation." It soon became clear that he wanted something in return. My hospital record said I was a Buddhist, a designation from long ago, when I had been in the hospital for some tests.

Some thirty years ago, I sat on a bus rolling through the mountains of New Mexico north of Taos. For several months, I'd been reading books on Buddhism and sporadically meditating. I felt like someone learning to swim by doing exercises on the riverbank. It was time to jump in. So I committed myself to a week's meditation retreat at Lama. As the time drew closer, I began to worry that I wasn't ready for such a drastic withdrawal. In Taos, the night before, a second margarita temporarily bolstered my resolve, and in the morning, having filled my pockets with energy bars, I boarded the bus to the unknown. As we headed north, however, my doubts about the venture grew.

At Lama, I thought I'd been right to worry. Experienced meditators were busily arranging mats and benches throughout the hall—settling in. Nervously, I claimed a spot along a back wall, which I held for the week. The days wore on. Boredom, sleepiness, aches and pains, and impatience for the end occasionally gave way to acceptance, peace, and even exhilaration. The last day, I felt calm and centered. On my way back to Houston, I stopped in Santa Fe, where I sat still for a while on a sun-drenched bench in the square. Time seemed to stop. No yesterday, no tomorrow. Just peace. But amid the bustle of travelers in the Albuquerque airport, peace started slipping away. Perhaps it couldn't flourish in my everyday world.

Still, my practice at home became steadier, and for several years, I returned to Lama for solitude, reflection, and rejuvenation. In time, however, my devotion to meditation faded. I no longer went on retreats, and I eventually stopped meditating altogether. Now, however, a computer remembered me as a Buddhist from the day of our meeting years before, and the minister took me for one.

As the minister understood it, for Buddhists there is no God. Where then, he asked, could I find comfort in my time of trouble? Didn't I feel alone?

I began by parroting Proust, bolstered by the teaching of my parents and an ancient Greek poet. Well, the illness had come to me alone. The path was mine alone to walk. Family and friends could ease the trek, and perhaps my doctors could lift some of its burdens, but only I would meet my fate. What I said next, however, came not from my French companion, but from me. Death might well wait around the next turn, but agonizing wouldn't chase it away. If I thought that moaning would scare off death, I'd devote my days to complaining. Or to praying, if that would do the trick. But wishes and fears regarding tomorrow are like leeches that would suck the present dry. They would desiccate the only life I had. He looked at me. He seemed ready to ask another question. But after a short silence, he put his hand tentatively on my ankle, and smiled weakly. Then he turned and left the room. He left me to wonder: Would my parents have taken this view? Did I believe what I had told him? Or had I simply wanted to sound brave?

Proust had told me to find my own wisdom. There it was. Yes, my body had been angry. Abused as it had been, it would never again be the same. But as Proust had observed, my body wasn't me. How, then, had I been scarred? In my mind? My feelings needn't be me either. Doubt, confusion, boredom, and exasperation, swirled in my mind. Yet peace could emerge from watching, not from clinging; from attention to this moment, not from absorption in what had been or what might be. I had to be my own teacher. I had to listen to my own brave words. I had to live the life they implied.

Day by day, I took up this challenge, as I might a candle, to illuminate the doings of my life. It wavered in inevitable moments of doubt and fear, but it never fully dimmed, even in the shadow of death. Today, stigmata testify to my body's suffering. I bear the marks borne by my mother and my uncle. I walk uneasily like my father. Loss of hair, skin blotches, stiffness, and newly prominent veins tell of a war within. As does my stooping posture, a consequence of so many steroids for so long. But a fragile truce now prevails. I often recall a banner from my Buddhist days. It told me how to tend the flame: "Be Here Now." So here I am with my family and friends, with my teaching and writing. Moment by moment...

And with Proust, who is again a good companion. He was right that on a journey like mine, there comes a time for even the best companion to step aside—for the traveler to go it alone. Now I'm glad to welcome him back. I continue to read his work with great pleasure, even though he continues to complain a lot. If he would listen to me, I could give him some good advice.

EPILOGUE

L eukemia and the ongoing consequences of its treatment have drawn tight the physical boundaries of my world—first in the hospital and now at home. But through my computer screen, I can still immerse myself in the rush of the virtual world. The pace of life in the high-speed lane of the digital age is unrelenting. So many happenings; so many claims on our attention. Earlier, I compared contemporary life to a vaudeville act in which the entertainer races from pole to pole to keep plates spinning atop them. We flit from one task to another, attending to the pressing demands of a host of digital entities in our technology-mediated life.

I have mostly retired my own vaudeville act. I devote more coherent attention to single subjects, one pole at a time. But I watch and wonder. Over five decades, I was deeply involved in various aspects of computing, beginning with artificial intelligence and clinical decision-making. Later, I became a professor and consultant to businesses on the development and management of computational resources. After so many years of connections with computing, I remain intrigued by its remarkable advance.

But what I need to know to live my life fully isn't to be found in the Eden of everything. Nor, I've discovered, does it lie in the pronouncements of my physicians. Modern medicine can plumb the depths of the body, but cannot uncover spirit or soul. And it is these I must marshal in the days to come, however many there may be.

What I need lies in the magical garden of the past. As I sit at my desk to finish this book, I see portals to that garden: ancient Greek poems and Buddhist sutras, writings by Proust, Woolf, and others, and especially some medals and an old shoebox. Often, I've found what Woolf promised—the present enriched by the backing of the past.

When I was ten, my parents and I ventured to a clothing store near a bridge that spanned the Hudson River, which marked the southern boundary of the town. A modest population such as ours could sustain only a few stores where clothes for a boy of ten could be found. I suspect my parents chose this one for its good balance of selection and price.

For me, their choice proved to be both exciting and unnerving. I was immediately drawn to an x-ray machine that was used to fit shoes. When I stood on its platform, much like weighing myself, I could peer down a tube to see my skeletal toes arrayed in my shoes. When I wiggled a toe, the image wiggled in concert. Presumably this x-ray vision improved shoe fitting, but for me, it was simply a marvel. So while my parents wandered through the store, I returned several times to study my ghostly toes there seen by the machine. The device gave me an intriguing new view of a part of me. Under the flesh, bones were working to enable my walking and running. I knew this, but I think that after seeing my feet in the machine, I never thought of them in quite the same way again.

The store gave me another new view of myself, one that proved disquieting. My parents had found some pants and a shirt for me. "Try them on," they urged. "Look at them in the mirror." Into the changing room I went. I shucked my t-shirt and shorts, donned the new apparel, as they say, and emerged to pose before the mirror. I remember neither the clothes nor my reaction to them. I think my parents found them suitable. I do, however, remember the mirror—or more precisely the mirrors, one in front and one on each side. By stepping forward, the customer could get a side view in addition to the ordinary facing view. When I stepped forward in my new clothes, I could see my profile, a view of myself I had never seen before. Head to toe, there I stood in side view. And I was mortified.

It was common for the kids I played with to attach nicknames to one another. Some stuck for a day or so; others for a long time. Occasionally, one that seemed to have faded away reemerged for uncertain reasons. Some nicknames derived from personal characteristics. Mousey was a little guy. BurpBurp had stomach problems. Blimpy was overweight. Baldy had hair problems. We never gave much thought to the feelings such names might have engendered in their recipients. And those named seldom complained. But I knew how it felt.

Two nicknames attached to me, each briefly, but for long enough to be discomforting. The first, Pinoke, was short for Pinocchio—for my nose. Not because I was a liar, but because my nose was seen as jutting out (and up?). The second, Tug, memorialized my way of walking in which my rear end apparently jutted out. Neither name stuck with the group, and in a month or so, each was forgotten by all—except me. From time to time, I worried. But I couldn't see these features, and so for the most part my embarrassment subsided.

Then the mirror brought the nicknames back. It showed why my playmates had noted my nose and rear end. There I was in profile, guilty as charged. I retreated from the mirrors and fled to the shoe machine. When my parents called me back to confirm the fitting, I approached the mirrors cautiously. Maybe I had made a mistake. I stepped slowly in. No, the same profile appeared.

Over the years, my unease concerning those particulars of my profile faded. But I now knew that my image of my body was an invention. Others didn't see my image of myself. A cause for worry arose. As I entered my teens, the judgment of peers assumed new prominence, leading to the obsessions of high school years and beyond. And I was not alone. My classmates worried about their looks. Careful with that lipstick, cover that blemish, slick down that cowlick, polish those nails, choose just the right clothes. Insofar as physical appearance was concerned, we could have joined Bing Crosby when he sang, "Accentuate the positive / Eliminate the negative / Latch on to the affirmative / Don't mess with Mister In-Between." We retained our membership in that chorus for years.

Of course, you can't judge a book by its cover, we are told. You must read a book to know its worth. You must somehow get behind appearances to read another, to know if that person could be a friend, a lover, a counselor, a mere acquaintance, or even an enemy. The magical machine in the department store revealed the inner structure and workings of bones. It saw through appearances. No matter what the shoe—fancy or plain— the machine revealed what lay within. Lacking such power, we often struggle to infer the feelings and motives that underlie observable behavior. Our way of assessing what lies beneath is seldom direct as in an x-ray image. Instead we create a picture that we refine and retouch in multiple encounters and with considerable reflection. But unlike foot bones that grow along predictable paths, personalities can go off in surprising and even distressing ways. In the digital world, where selves can be both constructed and fragmented and are often in flux, the challenge of knowing others—and even ourselves—can be great.

During my most recent stay in the hospital, I thought quite a bit about that long-ago visit to the department store. Now many machines peered into the workings of my body. Some are more powerful and precise analogs to the x-ray machine for shoe fitting. Others not even imagined in that time visualize not just the structure, but the functioning of my lungs, heart, and other organs as well. They seek to look behind the scenes, to watch for malfunction or malevolence not yet manifested in my outward appearance. They see me from perspectives well beyond the triptych of the department store.

I live today because of such machines. They read Proust's language of the body and intervene in its workings. But technology has not granted its bounty freely. I am decomposed into numbers, shadows, and lines in a kind of modernist painting. My doctors, connoisseurs of such art, seem to prefer this way of understanding me. A kind of Klee for a pulmonary function test, a Modigliani for an echo cardiogram, and a Pollock for the ever mysterious GVHD. But what about me? None of these portraits encompasses me. Where am I in this welter of number, tracings, and signals?

This is not a matter of vanity as it might have been in my teenage years. During my illness, I have dropped out of the chorus that urges me to accentuate positive and eliminate negative. First, I am in my seventies, and age has made marks which neither creams nor rinse can elide. And aggressive treatment of leukemia has blotched my skin, shrunk my muscles, and stooped my posture. No point in trying to hide what's happening to me. Yet in dropping my guard, in eschewing pretense, I have opened myself to welcoming warmth.

The touches of nurses and care assistants bring comfort and often relief. And despite our family's devotion to self-reliance, I am learning to ask for help. More remarkable has been the loss of modesty. Naked, I'm washed, wiped, creamed, and powdered by men and women, young and old. I put myself literally in their hands. And in this giving up of caution and protection, I've gained an ease I hadn't previously known. Are my legs sturdy, my arms strong, my chin firm, my posture strong? They know the answers as well as I do. I don't have to pretend. The hands welcome me as I truly am. It's a gift.

My head almost touches hers as she bends over my arm. With one hand, she holds my arm still. With two fingers of the other, she seems to caress it. She is looking for, feeling for a tracing beneath my skin, an artery she can penetrate with a sharp needle. Finding a good point of entry isn't easy. My arm is bruised and scarred from small accidents and many previous blood drawings. And a vein won't do. It's an artery she's after. She taps my arm as though to induce some response from an artery within. Tap, tap, tap. Over her shoulder, I watch intently, guessing whether one spot or another will be the site of the arterial blood draw.

I've had many, many venous blood draws. Find a vein, stick with a needle, and draw blood into one or more tubes for laboratory analysis. These draws are straightforward and seldom painful. At their worst, they are like an insect bite.

But assessing arterial blood gas is different. The needle goes deeper in search of an artery. Having pierced the skin, the needle's point probes within, seeking arterial blood. In the best of circumstances, the pain of the arterial penetration passes quickly, almost like a second, more vigorous insect bite. But when it punctures an artery, the sharp metal probe can cause a bright, intense flaring of pain. An obscene pain arising from within that can't be rubbed away. Thankfully, its flaring is brief, and as the stolen blood fills the tube, the hurt subsides. Soon, it is but a disembodied remembrance.

Of course, anticipating pain and remembering it are different matters. She remembers the patients who grimaced and shuddered, who cried out, even screamed, whose eyes watered. She is thinking about the pain she is about to inflict. She knows that with skill and luck on her part, the pain may be lessened. But as she searches for a site for the blood draw, she murmurs an anticipatory, "I'm sorry."

I, too, know the pain is coming. She has found her spot, and poised her needle. In the moment, she and I are collaborators. She must take, and I must give. Outside and inside coalesce. The searing pain seals the bond, creating a brief intimacy. The tube has filled. She breathes out and withdraws the needle. I relax the tension that had surreptitiously crept into me. She places my finger to press down on some gauze that she puts over the bright blood that marks the needle's exit. And quickly the ordinary returns. Wrapping the wound, which now has stopped bleeding, discarding used materials, labelling the tube of arterial blood. Nothing special now, just hospital routine. Nothing memorable. But I'll long remember the needle, the pain, and that brief, deeply personal connection.

Now, to finish this book, I recount one more way in which I see through the present to the depths of the past. With difficulty, I face myself in the mirror. It's not a psychological block that keeps me from looking at my image directly. Instead, my weakened spine keeps my head tilted downward. So daily I wash my hands and face and brush my teeth with little attention to the mirror. Every day or two, however, I accept the pain and stand straighter to contemplate my reflection for a minute or so. Then the mirror becomes a *pentimento* with my image overlaid on lines of the past.

When I was young, I couldn't see my resemblance to my father that others saw. Now much older, I've come to look like him in the years before his death. In the mirror, I see his ears flaring behind mine; his eyes similarly colored and placed; and his smile with roughly the same lift and span. As I stretch up to get a full view, I recognize another connection that the mirror cannot reveal. My father and I are linked by persistent pain: his from shrapnel in his leg; mine from fractures in my back.

Uncle George, too, shows through my image. Like his, my hair is patchy and tufted. Small flakes of skin sometimes lie scattered on my shoulders, reminding me of his dandruff. On my face are red blotches like those that marred his all his adult life. Again, there are connections the mirror can't capture. My step is shuffling, and my movements, stiff. And my use of oxygen adds to my talking a kind of huffing and puffing that accompanied his.

I step back and bring my arms up to reveal bruises and wounds. My mother becomes part of my reflection. For twenty years, cortisone for a recalcitrant pneumonia thinned her skin. Often a bandage marked the encounter of an arm or leg with the edge of a door, a branch, or even the paw of one of her beloved terriers. My skin, too, has been thinned—even more than hers—by my long course of steroids. I frequently tear it and always show wounds in different stages of healing. Even a modest blow can leave a garish red or purple bruise. For several years, a port three inches long thrust from my neck, a constant reminder of the ongoing struggle for control of my immune system. The foam cup pinned to her bathing suit for years memorialized her sacrifice of a breast and some lymph nodes to stem the advance of cancer.

I'm not a pretty picture. But when I look steadfastly at the mirror, I don't shrink from the aging, the reddened skin, and the wounds. In peace, I see through the present to the depths of the past. I ignore the stiffness. I put aside the pain. These are more than burdens. They are tokens of those who went before me. They connect me with my family across time. They are part of my story, not written on the page, but told in the language of the body. A story I read with my heart.